*I can do all things through Christ which strengtheneth me.*
*(Philippians 4:13 KJV)*

*I can do all things through Christ which strengtheneth me.*
*(Philippians 4:13 KJV)*

# Daily Devotions

## with

# Jen

*God Loves You . . . Turning to Jesus*

# JENNIFER TAYLOR

## Edited by Jennifer Skinnell

*I can do all things through Christ which strengtheneth me.*
*(Philippians 4:13 KJV)*
Copyright © Jennifer Taylor

*I can do all things through Christ which strengtheneth me.*
*(Philippians 4:13 KJV)*

## Dedication

I dedicate this book to my beloved and supportive church friends. Thank you for your love and support.

*I can do all things through Christ which strengtheneth me.*
*(Philippians 4:13 KJV)*

# Introduction

Devotions are defined as love, loyalty or enthusiasm for a person, activity, or group. With God's continuous love for us, it is necessary to devote our time and energy toward his teachings. *Daily Devotions with Jen* focuses on God's love and compassion for our world. Through prayer and daily reminders, we are able to refocus and create a more positive mindset. These reminders offer hope and a fresh renewal of our faith.

Create in me a clean heart, O God;
And renew a right spirit within me. (Psalm 51:10 KJV)

When you stop and think about how much of your time is spent on worry and doubt, is there any room left for peace and optimism? It is important to take time each day to rest and refocus your mind on God's purpose for your life. A helpful way to regain a positive outlook on your days is to read the Bible. Through scripture, we reconnect with God, his Son, and the Holy Spirit. Scripture transforms our hearts and minds by opening our souls to new beginnings.

Hast thou not known? Hast thou not heard, that the everlasting God, the Lord, the creator of the ends of the earth, fainteth not, neither is weary? There is no searching for his understanding. He giveth power to the faint; and to them that have no might he increaseth strength. Even the youths shall faint and be weary, and the young men shall utterly fall; But they that wait upon the Lord shall renew their strength; they shall mount up with wings as eagles; they shall run, and not be weary; and they shall walk, and not faint.
(Isaiah 40:28-31 KJV)

*I can do all things through Christ which strengtheneth me.*
*(Philippians 4:13 KJV)*

*Daily Devotions with Jen* provides scripture along with positive, yet straight forward reminders that you are loved and never alone. God's plan for your life is clearly written in his teachings and best followed on a daily basis.

Trust in the Lord with all thine heart; and lean not unto thine own understanding. In all thy ways acknowledge him, and he shall direct thy paths. (Proverbs 3:5-6 KJV)

*I can do all things through Christ which strengtheneth me.*
*(Philippians 4:13 KJV)*

## Preface

I have designed this book to be taken with you on your daily travels. The devotions in *Daily Devotions with Jen* are reminders of God's unfailing love for you. My devotions are designed to help you live your days full of hope and optimism. When in doubt, open *Daily Devotions with Jen* and take in God's Word. It will lift your spirits and leave you feeling full of gratitude!

*I can do all things through Christ which strengtheneth me.*
*(Philippians 4:13 KJV)*

# ♥Jesus Christ Is Our Living Hope♥

"For the believer there is hope beyond the grave, because Jesus Christ has opened the door to heaven for us by His death and resurrection." -Billy Graham

Hope saves us through the trials we face. How has hope in Jesus Christ saved you? It saved me through being a single mom of three young kids, loss of a job, death of a grandmother and friend, depression, and betrayal. Through hope and constant prayer, I was able to push through and began to see God at work.

Trust in the Lord with all your heart and lean not on your own understanding. (Proverbs 3:5 NIV)

Through him we have also obtained access by faith into this grace in which we stand, and we rejoice in hope of the glory of God. Not only that, but we rejoice in our sufferings, knowing that suffering produces endurance, and endurance produces character, and character produces hope, and hope does not put us to shame, because God's love has been poured into our hearts through the Holy Spirit who has been given to us. (Romans 5:2-5 NIV).

*~Hope Saves Us~*

*I can do all things through Christ which strengtheneth me.*
*(Philippians 4:13 KJV)*

# ♥ Stand Strong in the Lord ♥

Finally, be strong in the Lord and in the strength of his might. Put on the whole armor of God, that you may be able to stand against the schemes of the devil. For we do not wrestle against flesh and blood, but against the rulers, against the authorities, against the cosmic powers over this present darkness, against the spiritual forces of evil in the heavenly places. (Ephesians 6:10-12 ESV)

Some days are easier than others in terms of how strong we feel. Strength of mind, body, heart, and Spirit can find us at war with not only ourselves, but also with others. The deception of the devil can certainly control how we think, feel, and behave!

The real question is how are we responding to his deception? We have two choices. We can give in or we can stand strong in our Lord.

Think about how often you sweat the small stuff. This means getting upset if it rains, your kids get dirty, or you spill your coffee. Perhaps you trip over something or lose your keys. These are just a few examples, of course.

*I can do all things through Christ which strengtheneth me.*
*(Philippians 4:13 KJV)*

Do you remember to whom you belong and brush these little mishaps off your shoulder? If you let every single little thing upset you, then the devil wins.

Be watchful, stand firm in the faith, act like men, be strong. (1 Corinthians 16:13 ESV)

*~Be Strong and Courageous~*

# ❤Create a Relationship with God❤

If you want to know what your purpose is, then get to know your creator. God will never steer us wrong! It is us who typically choose a path without truly discerning if it is God's Will for us.

If anyone's will is to do God's will, he will know whether the teaching is from God or whether I am speaking on my own authority. (John 7:17 ESV)

Choose today to start fresh with our Lord! Pray, discern, trust Him, and His Will is your Will. A relationship with God is the best relationship you'll ever experience.

*~God Is for Everyone~*

*I can do all things through Christ which strengtheneth me.*
*(Philippians 4:13 KJV)*

## ♥*If I Spend My Last Breath Proclaiming Jesus, All Will Be Well*♥

Where's your focus? The news? Social media? Opinions and assumptions formed from baseless information? Or is your focus where it should be—on Jesus? He is the Alpha and Omega, the first and the last, the beginning and the end. People are just people! Jesus is King of Kings and Lord of Lords. He IS the Prince of Peace. Jesus is our salvation!

Jesus left the temple and was walking away when his disciples came up to him to call his attention to its buildings. 2 "Do you see all these things?" he asked. "I tell you the truth, not one stone here will be left on another; every one will be thrown down."

3 As Jesus was sitting on the Mount of Olives, the disciples came to him privately. "Tell us," they said, "when will this happen, and what will be the sign of your coming and of the end of the age?"

4 Jesus answered: "Watch out that no one deceives you. 5 For many will come in my name, claiming, 'I am the Messiah,' and will deceive many. 6 You will hear of wars and rumors of wars, but see to it that you are not alarmed. Such things must happen, but the end is still to come. 7 Nation will rise against nation, and kingdom against kingdom. There will be famines and earthquakes in various places. 8 All these are the beginning of birth pains.

9 "Then you will be handed over to be persecuted and put to death, and you will be hated by all nations because of me. 10 At that time many will turn away from the faith and will betray and hate each other, 11 and many false prophets will appear and deceive many people. 12 Because of the increase of wickedness, the love of most will grow cold, 13 but he who stands firm to the end will be saved. 14 And this gospel of the kingdom will be preached in the whole world as a testimony to all nations, and then the end will come.

15 "So when you see standing in the holy place 'the abomination that causes desolation,'[a] spoken of through the prophet Daniel—let the reader understand— 16 then let those who are in Judea flee

to the mountains. 17 Let no one on the roof of his house go down to take anything out of the house. 18 Let no one in the field go back to get his cloak. 19 How dreadful it will be in those days for pregnant women and nursing mothers! 20 Pray that your flight will not take place in winter or on the Sabbath. 21 For then there will be great distress, unequaled from the beginning of the world until now—and never to be equaled again.

22 "If those days had not been cut short, no one would survive, but for the sake of the elect those days will be shortened. 23 At that time if anyone says to you, 'Look, here is the Messiah!' or, 'There he is!' do not believe it. 24 For false messiahs and false prophets will appear and

*I can do all things through Christ which strengtheneth me.*
*(Philippians 4:13 KJV)*

perform great signs and wonders to deceive, if possible, even the elect. 25 See, I have told you ahead of time.

26 "So if anyone tells you, 'There he is, out in the desert,' do not go out; or, 'Here he is, in the inner rooms,' do not believe it. 27 For as lightning that comes from the east is visible even in the west, so will be the coming of the Son of Man. 28 Wherever there is a carcass, there the vultures will gather.

29 "Immediately after the distress of those days, the sun will be darkened, and the moon will not give its light; the stars will fall from the sky, and the heavenly bodies will be shaken.'[b] 30 "At that time the sign of the Son of Man will appear in the sky, and all the nations of the earth will mourn. 31 And he will send his angels with a loud trumpet call, and they will gather his elect from the four winds, from one end of the heavens to the other.

32 "Now learn this lesson from the fig tree: As soon as its twigs get tender and its leaves come out, you know that summer is near. 33 Even so, when you see all these things, you know that it is near, right at the door. 34 Truly I tell you, this generation will certainly not pass away until all these things have happened. 35 Heaven and earth will pass away, but my words will never pass away. (Matthew 24:1-35)

*~Jesus Is the Way~*

*I can do all things through Christ which strengtheneth me.*
*(Philippians 4:13 KJV)*

# ♥ Choose Praying Over Complaining ♥

Do not grumble against one another, brothers, so that you may not be judged; behold, the Judge is standing at the door. (James 5:9 ESV)

Rejoice always, pray continually, give thanks in all circumstances; for this is God's will for you in Christ Jesus. (1 Thessalonians 5:16-18 NIV)

Has complaining ever led to positive circumstances in your life? Or, has praying instead brought you peace? The difference is monumental! Always choose praying over complaining! Give your burdens to God and move on with your day. I, too, am reminded of this today. Rest in our Lord and change your mindset.

Do not be anxious about anything, but in every situation, by prayer and petition, with thanksgiving, present your requests to God. And the peace of God, which transcends all understanding, will guard your hearts and your minds in Christ Jesus. (Philippians 4:6-7 NIV)

*~Fight All Your Battles with Prayer, You Will Always Win~*

*I can do all things through Christ which strengtheneth me.*
*(Philippians 4:13 KJV)*

# ♥Wisdom Leads to Understanding the Truth♥

Let the wise hear and increase in learning, and the one who understands obtain guidance. (Proverbs 1:5 ESV)

Praying instead of complaining is wise!
Researching instead of believing everything you see at first glance is wise!
Doing good and not evil is wise!
Choosing self-control over arguing is wise!
Choosing Jesus over Satan is wise!
Following God's instruction over earthly instruction is wise!
Loving others, being kind, and communicating is wise!
Praying for wisdom and understanding is wise!
Read Proverbs for Truth, Wisdom and Understanding!
Reading the Bible is wise.

"Whoever trusts in his own mind is a fool, but he who walks in wisdom will be delivered."
(Proverbs 28:26 ESV)

*~Let Wisdom Rule Your Heart~*

*I can do all things through Christ which strengtheneth me.*
*(Philippians 4:13 KJV)*

# ♥ Wisdom in Truth ♥

"Trust in the Lord with all your heart, and do not lean on
your own understanding." (Proverbs 3:5 ESV)

The truth can hurt, but it will set us free! God's Word is
the truth. I'm re-reading Proverbs, and once again it is
opening my eyes.

Wisdom is the front runner here, and so is understanding
the difference between good and evil doings. Wisdom
allows us to conquer negative emotions. Fools give in to
the negativity and feed from its internal turmoil,
basically leaving us to "wrestle with ourselves".

Think of how often you've wrestled with anger,
bitterness, jealousy, resentment, hate, anxiety, fear, and
lust. I do not know one person who hasn't experienced
these soul-crushing emotions. But that's what they are—
soul crushing.

In Proverbs 3:5, God tells us to trust Him with all our
heart! Why would He say that if He didn't already love
us and have control of every situation we face? This is
God's truth—to have us trust Him in every situation and
not to trust our own emotions. This is actually wonderful
news! I for one do not want complete control. That
thought alone causes extreme anxiety in my heart.

*~Let Go and Let God~*

*I can do all things through Christ which strengtheneth me.*
*(Philippians 4:13 KJV)*

# ♥ My Prayer For You in 2020 ♥

I have been crucified with Christ. It is no longer I who live, but Christ who lives in me. And the life I now live in the flesh I live by faith in the Son of God, who loved me and gave Himself up for me.
(Galatians 2:20 ESV)

We grow where we are loved. Did you know that there is no greater love than the love of Jesus? If you have ever felt unwanted and lost, just know that Jesus' love is here for you. The whole point in God sending His only Son was to save us, and for us to know that His love is our love.

My prayer for you in 2020 is that you turn to Jesus, not because He wants to control you, but because His love leads you to eternal salvation.

*~Jesus Is Here for You~*

*I can do all things through Christ which strengtheneth me.*
*(Philippians 4:13 KJV)*

# ♥ Let Us Pray ♥

Do not be anxious about anything, but in every situation, by prayer and petition, with thanksgiving, present your requests to God. And the peace of God, which transcends all understanding, will guard your hearts and your minds in Christ Jesus. (Philippians 4:6-7 NIV)

Praying when we wake up first thing in the morning sets a positive tone for things to come. Prayer opens our hearts and releases the stresses that our minds continuously carry. I keep a prayer candle on my kitchen window sill. I light it and pray for all my burdens and your burdens to be taken away. This brings instant peace to my heart!

Therefore I tell you, whatever you ask for in prayer, believe that you have received it, and it will be yours. (Mark 11:24 NIV)

Therefore confess your sins to each other and pray for each other so that you may be healed. The prayer of a righteous person is powerful and effective. (James 5:16 NIV)

*~Pray Without Ceasing~*

*I can do all things through Christ which strengtheneth me.*
*(Philippians 4:13 KJV)*

## ♥ *Motivate One Another to do Good* ♥

And let us consider one another to provoke unto love
and to good works. (Hebrews 10:24 KJV)

I've seen people commit acts of evil and persuade others
to do the same. It's all over social media now and in the
music we listen to and in the movies we watch. I've
heard people joke about being sinners and laughingly
say they're going to hell. I never understood why
anyone would think that hell is funny and it's cool to go
there. Hell is very real! It's just as real as Heaven.

If we're given one life and a chance to turn to Jesus, we
must encourage more people to do just that!

Turn to Me and be saved, all the ends of the earth! For I
am God, and there is no other. (Isaiah 45:22 ESV)

In the devil there is no love, there's only deception.
Through Jesus, and only Jesus, will we fully understand
the love of God.

*~Go Out and Motivate Others to Do Good as Jesus has*
*Done~*

*I can do all things through Christ which strengtheneth me.*
*(Philippians 4:13 KJV)*

# ♥ Good will Come to You ♥

Submit to God and be at peace with him; in this way
prosperity will come to you. Accept instruction from his
mouth and lay up his words in your heart.
(Job 22:21-22 NIV)

I am happy to submit myself to our Lord and not to
anyone else or a false god. Good has come to my life
because of my loyalty and love for Him. I place my
complete trust and hope in our Lord in Heaven. He is
my rock, my foundation, and my home. I sleep better, I
breathe deeper, and I understand more about life now
than I ever did in my youth.

Turn to Me and be saved, all the ends of the earth; For I
am God, and there is no other. (Isaiah 45:22 NIV)

Being saved should be the most comforting thought
anyone should have. And it's so simple to achieve—
Jesus, repentance, no more sinning, and love!

Then he brought them out and said, "Sirs, what must I
do to be saved?" And they said, "Believe in the Lord
Jesus, and you will be saved, you and your household."
And they spoke the word of the Lord to him and to all
who were in his house. And he took them the same hour
of the night and washed their wounds; and he was
baptized at once, he and all his family."
(Acts 16:30-33 ESV)

*~It Is So Simple to Achieve~*

*I can do all things through Christ which strengtheneth me.*
*(Philippians 4:13 KJV)*

# ♥ There Is Freedom in Jesus Christ ♥

For you were called to freedom, brothers. Only do not use your freedom as an opportunity for the flesh, but through love serve one another. (Galatians 5:13 ESV)

Have you ever felt so bold that you were able accomplish things you deemed impossible? When we go out of our comfort zones and experience the joy that being brave offers, we create a new sense of freedom in our souls. This freedom allows us to show kindness, share the Word of God, and pray for others who need it most.

Now the Lord is the Spirit, and where the Spirit of the Lord is, there is freedom. (2 Corinthians 3:17 ESV)

Think about how you can be bold in the name of Jesus Christ! How are you being called? How can you go out and serve others as Christ has done?

*~We can All be Brave~*

# ♥ He Is Our Light ♥

I am the light of the world. Whoever follows me will not walk in darkness, but will have the light of life. (John 8:12 ESV)

I've noticed a huge change in my spirit since I acknowledged Jesus Christ as my savior! I find resolution to my struggles and help share His light with

*I can do all things through Christ which strengtheneth me.*
*(Philippians 4:13 KJV)*

those who need Him most. You too can feel His amazing glow that only He can provide! And this isn't just great news for some people, this is great news for everyone.

In the same way, let your light shine before others, so that they may see your good works and give glory to your Father who is in heaven. (Matthew 5:16 ESV)

*~Let Him Be Your Glow~*

# ❤*When I Am Afraid*❤

When I am afraid, I put my trust in you. In God, whose word I praise—in God I trust and am not afraid. What can mere mortals do to me? (Psalm 56:3-4 NIV)

We have nothing to fear but fear itself. Fear is a scheme that the devil stirs up in us so that he can conquer our emotions. But this is what our Lord tells us in these times of trouble...

Fear thou not; for I am with thee: be not dismayed; for I am thy God: I will strengthen thee; yea, I will help thee; yea, I will uphold thee with the right hand of my righteousness. (Isaiah 41:10 KJV)

*~Place Your Trust in our Lord*
*Place Your Worry in His Hands*
*Be at Peace in His Holy Name~*

*I can do all things through Christ which strengtheneth me.*
*(Philippians 4:13 KJV)*

# ♥There is no Shame in Following Jesus Christ♥

So everyone who acknowledges me before men, I also
will acknowledge before my Father who is in heaven,
but whoever denies me before men, I also will deny
before my Father who is in Heaven.
(Matthew 10:32-33 ESV)

I never fully understood what it meant to follow Jesus
until about three years ago. I started reading more
Scripture and writing more devotions about Him. When
I prayed, my mind was finally set on Him. When I
struggled with negative emotions and finances, I
reminded myself to keep Him as my center. He was the
only one bringing peace to my heart, and He was the
only one I found I could trust.

So faith comes from hearing, and hearing through the
word of Christ. (Romans 10:17 ESV)

We all struggle in this life! But with Jesus as our center,
we are able to push through with His love and hope.
Without Him, we will still struggle. Why not grab hold
of His love and constant being so the struggles are easily
overcome by His reminder of our salvation?

*~For I am Not Ashamed of the One Who Saved Me~*

*I can do all things through Christ which strengtheneth me.*
*(Philippians 4:13 KJV)*

## ♥After Christmas Joy♥

Trust in the LORD with all thine heart; and lean not
unto thine own understanding. (Proverbs 3:5 KJV)

Now, with another passing Christmas, how can we
continue to find joy in everyday living? I admit that I
woke up this morning feeling anxious over what this
next year will bring now that the focus of Christmas has
passed. The feeling of uncertainty and fear were the
front runners, but the Holy Spirit is always faithful in
reminding me to trust God! Proverbs 3:5 brings
immediate peace to my mixed emotions in every
situation.

If you're experiencing some post-Christmas blues, turn
to scripture. It's our guide to understanding that God is
in complete control, and we are here to live in joy,
peace, and love. There will be difficult moments where
it feels only natural that we should live in fear, but God
is great! His Will always prevails, and we are called to
trust Him.

*~Trust in the Lord~*

*I can do all things through Christ which strengtheneth me.*
*(Philippians 4:13 KJV)*

# ♥*Christmas Everyday*♥

For God so loved the world, that He gave His only Son,
that whoever believes in Him should not perish, but
have eternal life. (John 3:16 ESV)

My sweet daughter knows me so well. She filled my
stocking this past Christmas with the things I love
most—reminders of Jesus' love.

I hope and pray that everyone had a beautiful Christmas,
full of love, joy, and peace. It was Jesus who ensured
that we would live a life in abundance through His
sacrifice and love. And even though it's the day after
Christmas, we can still live like it's Christmas every
single day!

Let us continue to be kind, to give, to help, to love, to
forgive, and to be hopeful in every situation.

I have said these things to you, that in me you may have
peace. In the world you have tribulation, but take heart; I
have overcome the world. (John 16:33 ESV)

*~Continue to Go Out and Share His Love~*

*I can do all things through Christ which strengtheneth me.*
*(Philippians 4:13 KJV)*

# ♥For God or For You♥

The heart of man plans his way, but the Lord establishes
his steps. (Proverbs 16:9 ESV)

Sometimes in life, I think about what I'm doing for God
versus what I'm doing for myself. We must not get
caught up in using His Holy name as an excuse for us to
do whatever we want. If you decide to do things that He
has not personally requested of you, then take Him with
you and keep Him as your center in your personal
decision making!

His strength is your strength
His guidance will prevail on your journey
His love is with you through every adventure
Do not be anxious, trust in His timing
If you seek wisdom, let Him teach you
Pray and He will listen

The Lord will fulfill his purpose for me; your steadfast
love, O Lord, endures forever. Do not forsake the work
of your hands. (Psalm 138:8 ESV)

*~Teach Me to Do Thy Will~*

*I can do all things through Christ which strengtheneth me.*
*(Philippians 4:13 KJV)*

# ♥The Name Jesus♥

She will give birth to a son, and you are to give him the name Jesus,[a] because he will save his people from their sins." (Matthew 1:21 NIV)

What can I possibly say about Jesus that I haven't already said? Scripture often speaks for itself, which is why The Word of God has always been and will always be forever.

For unto us a child is born, unto us a son is given: and the government shall be upon his shoulder: and his name shall be called Wonderful, Counsellor, The mighty God, The everlasting Father, The Prince of Peace.
(Isaiah 9:6 KJV)

The birth of Christ was a gift for mankind. He was born of the Virgin Mary, who was chosen by our Lord out of love. He grew up a strong man of humility, wisdom, and grace. His sacrifice was out of love, and his legacy is our guidance through this life until He returns.

I am Alpha and Omega, the beginning and the ending, saith the Lord, which is, and which was, and which is to come, the Almighty. (Revelation 1:8 KJV)

*~Jesus~*

*I can do all things through Christ which strengtheneth me.*
*(Philippians 4:13 KJV)*

# ♥ Prayers for You ♥

And I will pray the Father, and he shall give you another
Comforter, that he may abide with you for ever.
(John 14:16 KJV)


Dear Heavenly Father,

I pray this day for those of your children struggling this
Christmas season. May you fill their hearts with hope
and help them to feel your loving arms around them. I
pray that all of your children live their days in good
health, joyful family moments, safe encounters, and
loving surroundings. In Jesus' name I pray, Amen


But the God of all grace, who hath called us unto his
eternal glory by Christ Jesus, after that ye have suffered
a while, make you perfect, stablish, strengthen, settle
you. (1 Peter 5:10 KJV)

*~God Bless You Always~*

*I can do all things through Christ which strengtheneth me.*
*(Philippians 4:13 KJV)*

# ♥ Titus 2:7 ♥

Show yourself in all respects to be a model of good
works, and in your teaching show integrity, dignity.
(Titus 2:7 ESV)

Unfortunately, we have a severe lack of integrity and
dignity in our midst. Those who say they dislike
slanderous behavior are proving to be even more
morally corrupt than their counterpart. The work of the
Devil is at hand. For nothing good comes from lying,
cheating, stealing, using vulgar language, and being
corrupt. We are called to love one another, not to
condemn one another.

I pray this day for our world that we may listen,
communicate, educate, and sow love instead of hate. I
pray that The Lord's truth prevails and that justice is
rightfully served to those who continue down the path of
unrighteousness.

"Love does not delight in evil but rejoices with the
truth." (1 Corinthians 13:6 NIV)

*~Do Not Let Evil Conquer You, But Conquer Evil by*
*Doing Good~*

*I can do all things through Christ which strengtheneth me.*
*(Philippians 4:13 KJV)*

# ❤️ Faith it Till You Make it ❤️

I pray that out of his glorious riches he may strengthen
you with power through his Spirit in your inner being,
so that Christ may dwell in your hearts through faith.
And I pray that you, being rooted and established in
love. (Ephesians 3:16-17 NIV)

Years ago, I went through what seemed like endless
dark moments. Things changed overnight for my family,
and then it continued into a downward spiral. Has this
happened to you? It seems impossible at times to
recover from your struggles, but there is always hope.

I knew that even during my hardships, I needed to pray.
I reminded myself to stay hopeful and to remain faithful
to God's promises. I basically faithed it until I made it in
life. I continued to work hard as a single mom and as a
faithful child of God. Then, God delivered!

Because you know that the testing of your faith produces
perseverance. (James 1:3 NIV)

*~Your Faith Can and Will Move Mountains in Your*
*Life~*

*I can do all things through Christ which strengtheneth me.*
*(Philippians 4:13 KJV)*

# ♥*Our Light*♥

Jesus will prevail! Always, now, and forever, He was the chosen one to save us. As Christmas Day approaches, let us reflect on the light He provides in our lives. He *is* the light in our darkness. He *is* love in a hateful world.

"The light shines in the darkness, and the darkness has not overcome it." (John 1:5 ESV)

Again Jesus spoke to them, saying, "I am the light of the world. Whoever follows me will not walk in darkness, but will have the light of life." (John 8:12 ESV)

I acknowledge Jesus as the light in my world. When I'm facing the challenges that life often presents, I turn to Him in prayer for guidance. I give thanks regularly, in addition to keeping Him on my mind in all that I do.

You may have heard the common phrase, "What would Jesus do?". Well, we are called to follow His example and to share the Word of God with all nations.

But you are a chosen race, a royal priesthood, a holy nation, a people for his own possession, that you may proclaim the excellencies of him who called you out of darkness into his marvelous light. (1 Peter 2:9 ESV)

*~Acknowledge His Light~*

*I can do all things through Christ which strengtheneth me.*
*(Philippians 4:13 KJV)*

# ♥ Not As the World Gives ♥

Peace I leave with you, my peace I give unto you: not as the world giveth, give I unto you. Let not your heart be troubled, neither let it be afraid. (John 14:27 KJV)

Finding peace through Jesus is like experiencing laughter through painful tears. I know this because this exact scenario happened to me. Imagine for a moment that your sadness is replaced with joyous peace in a matter of a second! This is what heartfelt prayer does for our souls; it opens our hearts to hearing His beautiful voice.

Whether people know it or not, we all need Jesus. His love is pure and His peace is not the sort of peace we obtain here on earth through worldly possessions. His peace heals.

Through my faith, He has healed my anxiety, depression, and stress. Through prayer and hope, I have been saved. Through prayer, broken family relationships have been mended. Through prayer, I have been able to put my complete trust in our Lord.

I have told you these things, so that in me you may have peace. In this world you will have trouble. But take heart! I have overcome the world. (John 16:33 NIV)

*~Jesus Leaves Us Peace~*

*I can do all things through Christ which strengtheneth me.*
*(Philippians 4:13 KJV)*

# ♥ Communication ♥

I tell you, on the day of judgment people will give
account for every careless word they speak.
(Matthew 12:36 ESV)

Good communication is a skill that must be taught.
Being able to communicate well is vital for all
relationships, whether they be work relationships,
friendships, or marriages. It is one of the most important
skills in life.

I sometimes struggle with what to say and sometimes
don't communicate when I should. Effective
communication requires more than an exchange of
information. It fosters understanding, strengthens
relationships, and builds trust.

There is always someone to share scripture with.
There is always someone to say "I love you" to.
There is always a time to give compliments.
There is always time to stop stressing and start loving.

Gracious words are like a honeycomb, sweetness to the
soul and health to the body. (Proverbs 16:24 ESV)

*~Open Your Hearts and Start Communicating~*

*I can do all things through Christ which strengtheneth me.*
*(Philippians 4:13 KJV)*

# ❤*What Brings You Joy*❤

Though you have not seen him, you love him; and even
though you do not see him now, you believe in him and
are filled with an inexpressible and glorious joy, for you
are receiving the end result of your faith, the salvation of
your souls. (1 Peter 1:8-9 NIV)

If there's love in your heart, it will feel like Christmas
all the time! Love brings joy, and joy brings love. For
me, this idea of love starts with Jesus. When we are able
to look to Him daily, we are able to find the joy of peace
we seek. There is no greater joy than keeping Jesus as
your center.

I delight greatly in the Lord; my soul rejoices in my
God. For he has clothed me with garments of salvation
and arrayed me in a robe of his righteousness, as a
bridegroom adorns his head like a priest, and as a bride
adorns herself with her jewels. (Isaiah 61:10 NIV)

*~The Joy of the Lord Is Your Strength~*

*I can do all things through Christ which strengtheneth me.*
*(Philippians 4:13 KJV)*

# ❤*Baptism*❤

And now what are you waiting for? Get up, be baptized
and wash your sins away, calling on his name.
(Acts 22:16 NIV)

Baptism is a beautiful form of devotion. It is an outward
act that symbolizes the inward phenomenon of coming
to and accepting Jesus Christ as real, as God incarnate,
as the sacrificial means by which those who believe in
him can be forever reconciled to God. The purpose of
baptism is to give visual testimony of our commitment
to Christ. It is the first step of discipleship.

The symbolism of baptism is that, just as Christ died and
was buried, so the baptized person is submerged
(whether physically or symbolically) under water. And
just as Christ rose again from beneath the earth, so the
baptized person rises again from beneath the water.
Under the water is the believer's old, dead, heavy,
suffocating life. Out of the water, cleansed by the blood
of Christ, is the believer's new, fresh, purposeful life.

Peter replied, "Repent and be baptized, every one of
you, in the name of Jesus Christ for the forgiveness of
your sins. And you will receive the gift of the Holy
Spirit." (Acts 2:38 NIV)

*~Start Fresh with Baptism~*

*I can do all things through Christ which strengtheneth me.*
*(Philippians 4:13 KJV)*

# ❤ Ready to Go ❤

Satisfy us in the morning with your unfailing love, that
we may sing for joy and be glad all our days.
(Psalm 90:14 NIV)

I'm waking with excitement in my heart and a smile on
my face! It's a beautiful crisp Sunday morning with the
sun peeking over the horizon. Christmas lights are
twinkling and the aroma of coffee is filling the house.

As I sit here thinking about church, I am reminded that
God's Word is a beautiful reminder of love, humility,
peace, and of helping others. His Word is also a
reminder that we are to live a life of service and joy. I
pray that you are also waking up with a joyful heart.

Let the morning bring me word of your unfailing love,
for I have put my trust in you. Show me the way I
should go, for to you I entrust my life.
(Psalm 143:8 NIV)

*~Good Morning, God Bless You, and Have a Joyous*
*Day~*

*I can do all things through Christ which strengtheneth me.*
*(Philippians 4:13 KJV)*

# ♥ It Saves Lives ♥

Do nothing from selfish ambition or conceit, but in
humility count others more significant than yourselves.
Let each of you look not only to his own interests, but
also to the interests of others.
(Philippians 2:3-4 ESV)

Praying for other people is an enormously loving gift!
Prayer is taking time out of our busy schedules to lift up
others and their needs to our Lord. When we pray for
others, including our enemies, we pray that God will
work in their lives. Think of a time when you prayed for
someone else and their situation improved. How did it
make them and you feel?

Therefore he is able also to save completely those who
come to God through him, because he always lives to
intercede for them. (Hebrews 7:25 NIV)

*~Pray for Others Today~*

*I can do all things through Christ which strengtheneth me.*
*(Philippians 4:13 KJV)*

# ♥ *Be Saved* ♥

That if thou shalt confess with thy mouth the Lord Jesus, and shalt believe in thine heart that God hath raised him from the dead, thou shalt be saved. (Romans 10:9 KJV)

Confess with your mouth; believe with your heart. I've always found it bewildering why many people see repentance as a threat. I see it as a beautiful gift. I love knowing that I do not have to control everything around me.

I used to think I had to, until I spoke to our Lord in prayer and asked Him to take my anxiety and worry away! I have confessed my sins, and I'm here to tell everyone that it is liberating. God is not here to see us fail; He's here to guide us to a fuller way of living. And that way of living is through His Son Jesus Christ.

If we confess our sins, he is faithful and just to forgive us our sins and to cleanse us from all unrighteousness. (1 John 1:9 ESV)

*~Repentance Leads to Freedom~*

*I can do all things through Christ which strengtheneth me.*
*(Philippians 4:13 KJV)*

# ♥ Fasting for a Purpose ♥

But he answered, "It is written, "'Man shall not live by bread alone, but by every word that comes from the mouth of God.'" (Matthew 4:4 ESV)

Since 2018, I have had this overwhelming feeling that I needed to start fasting. When I tried on a Sunday, I made it to 3pm, but was starving so I gave into temptation and ate.

Then, the next Sunday, I tried again and succeeded. I felt amazing and proud of myself the next morning. But I did not continue to fast. You see, I was fasting because the Bible said to. However, I wasn't doing it for Jesus, I was doing it for myself.

Fasting just to lose weight can be dangerous, and I was weak and dizzy. After more study, I now understand that Biblical fasting is avoiding temptation and being in Spirit with Jesus. His strength is our strength!

I'm now on week three of fasting on Sundays, but I'm also fasting today because my heart is convicted! I now understand the truth of how fasting brings me closer to God through prayer and avoiding the devil's temptation.

Scripture doesn't tell us "if" we fast, it explains "when" we fast. As Christians, fasting is a powerful form of worship that is part of our Spiritual journey.And when you fast, do not look gloomy like the hypocrites, for they disfigure their faces that their fasting may be seen

*I can do all things through Christ which strengtheneth me.*
*(Philippians 4:13 KJV)*

by others. Truly, I say to you, they have received their reward. But when you fast, anoint your head and wash your face that your fasting may not be seen by others but by your Father who is in secret. And your Father who sees in secret will reward you. (Matthew 6:16-18 ESV)

*~Fasting Creates an Increase of the Holy Spirit~*

# ♥ Fix Your Eyes on Jesus ♥

Looking unto Jesus the author and finisher of our faith; who for the joy that was set before him endured the cross, despising the shame, and is set down at the right hand of the throne of God. (Hebrews 12:2 KJV)

How is it possible to keep our eyes on Jesus with so much going on in our busy lives?! Well, it is possible. Jesus is not the one who over-plans, overthinks, and causes stress in our days—we are the cause. He is meant to be our safe place. Jesus is our peace through our storms! Jesus is our knight in shining armor! Jesus is our center.

For to us a child is born, to us a son is given, and the government will be on his shoulders. And he will be called Wonderful Counselor, Mighty God, Everlasting Father, Prince of Peace. (Isaiah 9:6 NIV)

*~Let Jesus Be Your Peace~*

*I can do all things through Christ which strengtheneth me.*
*(Philippians 4:13 KJV)*

## ❤ *Compassion through Prayer* ❤

Likewise the Spirit helps us in our weakness. For we do not know what to pray for as we ought, but the Spirit himself intercedes for us with groanings too deep for words. And he who searches hearts knows what is the mind of the Spirit, because the Spirit intercedes for the saints according to the will of God.
(Romans 8:26-27 ESV)

Loving our enemies is rather difficult at times. What I have found that works is to pray for them. Prayer is powerful, and when we exude heartfelt concern for those who have offended us, God will intercede. Pray that they forgive, that they humble themselves, that they learn how to love, and that they turn to Jesus.

Show compassion always through prayer, words, and thoughts! Difficult? Yes, it is, but it's necessary to do this as brothers and sisters in Christ.

*~Pray for Your Enemies~*

*I can do all things through Christ which strengtheneth me.*
*(Philippians 4:13 KJV)*

# ♥ One Common Denominator ♥

You, dear children, are from God and have overcome them, because the one who is in you is greater than the one who is in the world. (1 John 4:4 NIV)

Everyone's story is different. Everyone's pain is a struggle. But we all have one common denominator, and that is Jesus! We place our hope and trust in the Lord to overcome these hardships we face daily. We look to Him for guidance and grace. His love is our love! His forgiveness is our forgiveness! His Word is our Word.

Cast your worries to Him and be joyous! Jesus didn't die for us to live in sin and to live in a constant state of sadness. He died so that we could live and live life in abundance! By prayer and through our joy, we can live with Jesus as our constant reminder of love, patience, and joy.

I consider that our present sufferings are not worth comparing with the glory that will be revealed in us. (Romans 8:18 NIV)

*~The Struggle is Part of the Story~*

*I can do all things through Christ which strengtheneth me.*
*(Philippians 4:13 KJV)*


# ❤ *Look* ❤

You will seek me and find me when you seek me with
all your heart. (Jeremiah 29:13 ESV)

You, God, are my God, earnestly I seek you; I thirst for
you, my whole being longs for you.
(Psalm 63:1 NIV)

Ask and it will be given to you; seek and you will find;
knock and it will be opened to you. (Matthew 7:7 ESV)

I sought the Lord, and he answered me; and delivered
me from all my fears. (Psalm 34:4 ESV)

For the Son of Man came to seek and to save the lost.
(Luke 19:10 ESV)

Looking to Jesus, the founder and perfecter of our faith,
who for the joy was set before him endured the cross,
despising the shame, and is seated at the right hand of
the throne of God. (Hebrews 12:2 ESV)

*~Seek Him with all your heart!*
*Pray to Him with genuine concern and thanksgiving!*
*Love Him as He has loved you~*

*I can do all things through Christ which strengtheneth me.*
*(Philippians 4:13 KJV)*

## ❤ To Whom Do We Belong ❤

For if we live, we live to the Lord, and if we die, we die to the Lord. So then, whether we live or whether we die, we are the Lord's. (Romans 14:8 ESV)

There is so much going on in our world that it's tough sometimes to remember that we belong to God and not to man. New religions, such as new age thinking and spiritual deception, have entered our world and have taken over millions of hearts and minds. There is one God, one Jesus Christ, and one Holy Spirit, and they are all found in The Bible.

See what kind of love the Father has given to us, that we should be called children of God; and so we are. The reason why the world does not know us is that it did not know him. Beloved, we are God's children now, and what we will be has not yet appeared; but we know that when he appears we shall be like him, because we shall see him as he is. And everyone who thus hopes in him purifies himself as he is pure. (1 John 3:1-4 ESV)

Jesus is the same yesterday, today, and tomorrow. He is the reason we live and the reason we have salvation. Placing your faith in Him will never be the wrong answer; for it is to Him that we belong.

*~When We Belong to Jesus, We are Loved Forever~*

*I can do all things through Christ which strengtheneth me.*
*(Philippians 4:13 KJV)*

## ❤*Give Thanks*❤

All this is for your benefit, so that the grace that is
reaching more and more people may cause thanksgiving
to overflow to the glory of God.
(2 Corinthians 4:15 NIV)

I am so incredibly grateful for our Lord! His love, grace,
mercy, commandments, and blessings are unmeasurable.
Praise the Lord and His amazing ways!

Give thanks to the Lord, for he is good; his love endures
forever. (1 Chronicles 16:34 NIV)

Let us come before him with thanksgiving and extol him
with music and song. For the Lord is the great God, the
great King above all gods. (Psalm 95:2-3 NIV)

*~Our Lord Is Great~*

## ❤*What to Do*❤

Devote yourselves to prayer, being watchful and
thankful. (Colossians 4:2 NIV)

What do you do when you don't know what to do? I
absolutely go into prayer! My first reaction in any
situation is to seek God's Word. Discernment plays a
large roll in finding the proper direction to take. This
means judging a situation well before proceeding.

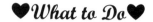

*I can do all things through Christ which strengtheneth me.*
*(Philippians 4:13 KJV)*

Do not be anxious about anything, but in every situation, by prayer and petition, with thanksgiving, present your requests to God. And the peace of God, which transcends all understanding, will guard your hearts and your minds in Christ Jesus. (Philippians 4:6-7 NIV)

*~Pray, Discern and Listen~*

# ❤ He Fills Our Cups ❤

May the God of hope fill you with all joy and peace as you trust in him, so that you may overflow with hope by the power of the Holy Spirit. (Romans 15:13 NIV)

More often than not, we take our blessings for granted. However, when we open our hearts to our Lord, His love and hope fill our souls. He fills our lives with contentment through His Word. Our hope in His timing and trust in His promises sustain us through what might seem like mundane days.

Our cups run over with His promises! We are filled abundantly by His love!

The thief comes only to steal and kill and destroy. I came that they may have life and have it abundantly. (John 10:10 ESV)

*~Open Your Hearts~*

*I can do all things through Christ which strengtheneth me.*
*(Philippians 4:13 KJV)*

# ❤*YOLO*❤

But if serving the LORD seems undesirable to you, then
choose for yourselves this day whom you will serve,
whether the gods your ancestors served beyond the
Euphrates, or the gods of the Amorites, in whose land
you are living. But as for me and my household, we will
serve the LORD." (Joshua 24:14 NIV)

The phrase "you only live once", otherwise known as
YOLO, brings several questions to my mind. If we were
blessed to live just once, then why live in constant sin
and temporary gratification? If we've been taught
through Scripture that our salvation only lies through
Jesus Christ, wouldn't people want that? Why not take
this phrase "yolo" to do the best you can according the
Christ?

His teachings, His love, and His promises should lead us
to the greatest place we'll ever know! But we get a
choice. Choose Jesus or choose the sin that the Devil
lays before us.

No one who abides in him keeps on sinning; no one who
keeps on sinning has either seen him or known him.
Little children, let no one deceive you. Whoever
practices righteousness is righteous, as he is righteous.
(1 John 3:6-7 ESV)

*~Choose Jesus over Sin~*

*I can do all things through Christ which strengtheneth me.*
*(Philippians 4:13 KJV)*

# ❤*All Things*❤

Did you know that through Jesus Christ you can accomplish anything? You can overcome any and all hardships that life places in front of you.

His strength is your strength!
His love is your love!
His patience is your patience!
His humility is your humility!
His courage is your courage!
His forgiveness is your forgiveness!
His trust in God is your trust in God!
His truth is your truth!
His God is your God!

I Can do all things through him who strengthens me.
(Philippians 4:13 ESV)

*~Jesus Christ is Our Hope and Salvation~*

*I can do all things through Christ which strengtheneth me.*
*(Philippians 4:13 KJV)*

# ♥*It Will Come Back Upon You*♥

Do not be deceived: God cannot be mocked. A man
reaps what he sows. (Galatians 6:7 NIV)

As a child of God, what are you putting out into the
world? How are you representing Christ Jesus? For
everything is seen by God! Your thoughts, your actions,
or lack thereof, will not go unnoticed. Everything we say
and do is taken into account and represents us as
Christians.

The eyes of the Lord are in every place, keeping watch
on the evil and the good. (Proverbs 15:3 ESV)

Can a man hide himself in secret places so that I cannot
see him? declares the Lord. Do I not fill heaven and
earth? declares the Lord. (Jeremiah 23:24 ESV)

Let us go out and sow seeds of love, humility, kindness,
forgiveness, truth, faith, patience, prayer, and
repentance.

*~We Will Reap What We Sow~*

*I can do all things through Christ which strengtheneth me.*
*(Philippians 4:13 KJV)*

# ♥God Needs to Be the Strength of Our Hearts♥

My flesh and my heart faileth: but God is the strength of my heart, and my portion for ever. (Psalm 73:26 KJV)

If you think for a moment about the word *forever*, how long does that actually mean? In other words, there isn't a finite amount of time that God will be with us. He is our portion forever, throughout all of eternity. His love is never ending! Now think for a moment about how much you love God. Is your love forever, eternal, and never ending for Him?

Our Lord is our strength and our comforter. We are called to express our need for His guidance along with the need for His grace. Call upon Him in your time of despair, your time of sorrow, and your time of giving thanks.

For You, Lord, are good, and forgiving, abounding in steadfast love to all who call upon you.
(Psalm 86:5 ESV)

*~Courage and Strength~*

*I can do all things through Christ which strengtheneth me.*
*(Philippians 4:13 KJV)*

# ♥ Hold Hands Not Grudges ♥

For the anger of man does not produce the righteousness
of God. (James 1:20 ESV)

Let go of the bitterness
Let go of the anger
Let go of the resentment
Let go of the grudges
Let go of the selfishness
Let go of the pride
Let go of the judging...


Be filled with the Holy Spirit
Be filled with patience
Be filled with forgiveness
Be filled with kindness
Be filled with love
Be filled with understanding
Be filled with humility
Be filled with Jesus.

Whoever is slow to anger has great understanding.
(Proverbs 14:29 ESV)

*~Instead, Love Another~*

*I can do all things through Christ which strengtheneth me.*
*(Philippians 4:13 KJV)*

# ❤Be A Prayer Warrior❤

Finally, my brethren, be strong in the Lord, and in the power of his might. (Ephesians 6:10 KJV)

Being active in prayer changes us from meek to mighty! Relying on the strength of our Lord rejuvenates our souls and revives our faith in His Holy plans. His strength is our strength! His love is our love! His courage is our courage!

Put on the whole armour of God, that ye may be able to stand against the wiles of the devil.
(Ephesians 6:11 KJV)

Pray for strength.
Pray for your families.
Pray for your churches.
Pray for your enemies.
Pray in every situation.

Confess your faults one to another, and pray for one another, that ye may be healed. The effectual fervent prayer of a righteous man availeth much.
(James 5:16 KJV)

*~Armor of God ~*

# ♥ *John 14:27* ♥

Peace I leave with, my peace I give unto you: not as the world giveth, give I unto you. Let not your heart be troubled, neither let it be afraid. (John 14:27 KJV)

If Jesus has worked miracles in your life and has opened your eyes to the goodness of our Lord, then how are you sharing that gift with others? We can go through tribulations and see that Jesus is the light in our darkness, but as His disciples, we are to follow His example and be the light for others who face constant battles. We are called to not let our hearts be troubled.

But what if people we know don't believe in Christ? How do we help them? We must first pray, then acknowledge the fact that Jesus was patient in His teachings. His soul was flooded with humility, wisdom, and forgiveness. We too are called to teach as Jesus taught.

The peace of Christ is like no other! It is a blessing; a gift. Let not your hearts be troubled! Go out and help others just as Christ has helped you. God tells us to not be anxious or afraid. This goes hand in hand with speaking on His behalf! We are not to be afraid to speak of His truth and love.

*~Be the Lion God Created You to Be~*

*I can do all things through Christ which strengtheneth me.*
*(Philippians 4:13 KJV)*

# ♥*You Shall Not Fear*♥

The Lord is my light and my salvation; whom shall I
fear? The Lord is the strength of my life; of whom shall
I be afraid? (Psalm 27:1 KJV)

You shall fear no one!
You shall fear no work conflict!
You shall fear no illness!
You shall fear no parenting stress!
You shall fear no new beginnings!
You shall fear no anxieties!
You shall fear no evil!
You shall fear no fear!

Walk in the light of the Lord, for He is your rock and
salvation! In Him, you shall live fearless in all you do
according to His Will.

*~Say No to Fear~*

*I can do all things through Christ which strengtheneth me.*
*(Philippians 4:13 KJV)*

# ♥ Lead or Follow ♥

For to this you have been called, because Christ also suffered for you, leaving you an example, so that you might follow in his steps. (1 Peter 2:21 ESV)

I often wonder how far people are willing to go to follow the crowd. But which crowd? For our salvation does not lie with humans, it is obtained through Christ and Christ alone. Are you willing to step out of the line and bear your cross?

And he said to all, "If anyone would come after me, let him deny himself and take up his cross daily and follow me." (Luke 9:23 ESV)

Willingly upholding the truth will be a tough venture but a worthy one! The opinions that God has for us far outweigh those of our fellow man. Be bold, be brave, and be a loyal servant of Christ.

As obedient children, do not be conformed to the passions of your former ignorance, but as he who called you is holy, you also be holy in all your conduct, since it is written, "You shall be holy, for I am holy."
(1 Peter 1:14-16 ESV)

*~Pray for Guidance~*

*I can do all things through Christ which strengtheneth me.*
*(Philippians 4:13 KJV)*

# ❤ Problems Don't Define You ❤

No temptation has overtaken you that is not common to man. God is faithful, and he will not let you be tempted beyond your ability, but with the temptation he will also provide the way of escape, that you may be able to endure it. (1 Corinthians 10:13 ESV)

Lessons learned! Don't be tempted to become angry when things do not go your way. When I face a tough situation, I'm immediately reminded to be slow to anger and quick to forgive.

Know this, my beloved brothers: let every person be quick to hear, slow to speak, slow to anger.
(James 1:19 ESV)

In any situation, it's important to remember that God is bigger than the hardships we face. Take time to pray, breathe, and know that you are never alone through your struggles!

It is the Lord who goes before you. He will be with you; he will not leave you or forsake you. Do not fear or be dismayed. (Deuteronomy 31:8 ESV)

*~God is Bigger than Our Problems~*

*I can do all things through Christ which strengtheneth me.*
*(Philippians 4:13 KJV)*

# ♥ What Is Grace ♥

Let us therefore come boldly unto the throne of grace,
that we may obtain mercy, and find grace to help in time
of need. (Hebrews 4:16 KJV)

"Grace" is a constant theme in the Bible, and it
culminates in the New Testament with the coming of
Jesus. The word "grace" is translated in the New
Testament coming from the Greek word *charis*, which
means "favor, blessing, or kindness."

We can all extend grace to others, but when the word
"grace" is used in connection with God, it takes on a
more powerful meaning. Grace is God choosing to bless
us rather than curse us as our sin deserves. It is His
benevolence to the undeserving.

Have we truly been able to show grace toward others
who live a life different from our own? The idea of
showing forgiveness, kindness, and patience toward
those who conduct negative behavior seems to be a
constant challenge. But grace is ours to spread to those
in need of redirection!

"But God, who is rich in mercy, for his great love
wherewith he loved us, even when we were dead in sin,
hath quickened us together with Christ, by grace ye are
saved." (Ephesians 2:4-5 KJV)

*~Sow Grace, Not Judgment~*

*I can do all things through Christ which strengtheneth me.*
*(Philippians 4:13 KJV)*

## ♥ The Distances We Go To ♥

But just as we have been approved by God to be
entrusted with the Gospel, so we speak, not to please
man, but to please God who tests our hearts.
(1 Thessalonians 2:4 ESV)

In an endlessly busy world, why do we seem to go the
distance to overly please other people? I have found that
my mission is to please God by sharing His Word,
helping others, and standing firm in my faith. I found it
stressful and unending trying to appease the needs of
others who take advantage of kindness. So how are you
pleasing God? How can we all please Him?

For am I now seeking the approval of man, or of God?
Or am I trying to please man? If I were still trying to
please man, I would not be a servant of Christ.
(Galatians 1:10 ESV)

What if instead, we went the distance in life for God? It
is an exciting journey full of mystery and unplanned
moments that God turns into blessings.

And without faith it is impossible to please him, for
whoever would draw near to God must believe that he
exists and that he rewards those who seek him.
(Hebrews 11:6 ESV)

*~If God is Pleased Then Stop Worrying About Who
Isn't~*

*I can do all things through Christ which strengtheneth me.*
*(Philippians 4:13 KJV)*

# ❤*Children of God*❤

Yet to all who did receive him, to those who believed in
his name, he gave the right to become children of God.
(John 1:12 NIV)

Dear Heavenly Father,

I pray this day for those who are lost and living without
faith. I pray for the souls of the abandoned, abused,
misled, and unholy to turn to Jesus for love, forgiveness,
and knowledge. I pray that everyone understands that
they are children of God and God alone. Through your
Word, love, and loyalty, please fill everyone's hearts
with the Holy Spirit. In Jesus' name I pray, Amen

*~You are a Child of God~*

# ❤*Branching Out*❤

"Family: like the branches on a tree, we all grow in
different directions, yet our roots remain as one."

The author of this statement is unknown, but they speak
the truth. We are born, we grow, we leave, and then
what? During this Holiday season, restore your faith and
hearts in the love of your families. Whether you're in a
loving family or a strenuous situation, forgiveness and
love are the recipes to repairing and building new family
ties.

*I can do all things through Christ which strengtheneth me.*
*(Philippians 4:13 KJV)*

"We love because he first loved us." (1 John 4:19 ESV)

Let your faith and hope in our Lord bring you closer than ever to your roots. Rekindle, reconnect, and rejoice in the love that this time of year brings!

Anyone who does not provide for their relatives, and especially for their own household, has denied the faith and is worse than an unbeliever. (1 Timothy 5:8 NIV)

*~Family and Faith are Forever~*

# ♥ We Are All Examples ♥

Do your best to present yourself to God as one approved, a worker who has no need to be ashamed, rightly handling the word of truth.
(2 Timothy 2:15 ESV)

Did you know that you're a minister of God's Holy Word? We are all created from His love, which leads us to teach on His behalf. His truth, His love, and His Word are for you, me, and everyone we meet!

Go out and be a servant of His love and truth. Share the Bible with friends and family. Be His number one supporter, because He is always rooting for you.

*~Start Your Ministry Today~*

*I can do all things through Christ which strengtheneth me.*
*(Philippians 4:13 KJV)*

## ♥ Be In Peace ♥

A little one shall become a thousand, and a small one a strong nation: I the Lord will hasten it in his time.
(Isaiah 60:22 KJV)

We too often try to control everything that happens in our world. We tend to take the stress of others' hardships on our own shoulders. But what happens when we take a step back and recognize that our God is bigger than our problems? By means of Prayer, Faith, and Trust, we are able understand that God has always and will forever be in control!

Many are the plans in the mind of a man, but it is the purpose of the Lord that will stand.
(Proverbs 19:21 ESV)

Let God have control so that you can live in peace.

But Jesus looked at them and said, "With man this is impossible, but with God all things are possible."
(Matthew 19:26 ESV)

*~Be Blessed, Not Stressed~*

*I can do all things through Christ which strengtheneth me.*
*(Philippians 4:13 KJV)*

# ♥Jesus's Road Take Me Home♥

Then Jesus told his disciples, "If anyone would come after me, let him deny himself and take up his cross and follow me." (Matthew 16:24 ESV)

An easy road it is not, but a worthy road it is indeed! My home is with my savior. Many times, I'm questioned on my intentions and on who Jesus is. To this I simply say, "Jesus is everything."

Again Jesus spoke to them, saying, "I am the light of the world. Whoever follows me will not walk in darkness, but will have the light of life." (John 8:12 ESV)

He is my center, my peace, my friend, and my helper through my struggles. My faith in Jesus Christ has opened my eyes to truth, light, and joy.

Jesus said to him, "I am the way, the truth, and the life. No one comes to the Father except through me." (John 14:6 ESV)

*~Follow Jesus, You'll Never Regret It~*

*I can do all things through Christ which strengtheneth me.*
*(Philippians 4:13 KJV)*

# ♥ Lift Up Your Eyes to the Heavens ♥

Lift up your eyes and look to the Heavens: Who created all these? He who brings out the starry host one by one and calls forth each of them by name. Because of his great power and mighty strength, not one of them is missing. (Isaiah 40:26 NIV)

Think about how often we walk with our eyes looking down. We do this to make sure we see what's right in front of us, and of course to make sure we don't trip and fall over something. But what happens when we look up while walking? Will we fall? Maybe! But we all fall down sometimes. Looking up brings new life to our eyes—a large, vast blue sky with endless clouds, birds, and beauty.

When we go through life only looking down, we only see what is directly in front of us. When we look up, we see endless possibilities of what the sky brings.
Our faith is the same as the direction we are looking. Spiritually looking down limits our faith, while looking up widens our faith to what God has to offer us!

Have you heard the phrase, "When in doubt, look up"? How many times a day do you have doubts?

Don't limit God's ability to do great things in your life by only looking down.

*~Trust in Your Spiritual Steps~*

*I can do all things through Christ which strengtheneth me.*
*(Philippians 4:13 KJV)*

# ❤ Jt Loves You ❤

I asked my sons this morning what I should write my morning devotion about. Jt, my five-year-old, immediately answered "Jt loves you"! Well here we are now talking about loving our neighbors as we love ourselves. It truly amazes me that my five-year-old chooses to love!

The second is this, "You shall love your neighbor as yourself." There is no other commandment greater than these. (Mark 12:31 ESV)

Our children are vulnerable to every influence they encounter. Because of our direction, they will either grow up to hate or to love others. As parents and children of God, we are properly commanded to love our neighbors. This does not just mean the people who live next door! This means we love all people as we are called to be as brothers and sisters in Christ.

Think about how you might and might not be loving others as we have been commanded to do. We are called to judge against sin righteously yet to love unconditionally! Pray for everyone, even those who offend you. Shake hands and share a smile with those who object to your views on faith. Lead by Christ's example of forgiveness and humility. And above all else, love as God loves you.

This is my commandment, that you love one another as I have loved you. (John 15:12 ESV)

*~Love Your Neighbor Also~*

*I can do all things through Christ which strengtheneth me.*
*(Philippians 4:13 KJV)*

# ❤Faith Gives Us Strength❤

I pray that out of his glorious riches he may strengthen
you with power through his Spirit in your inner being,
so that Christ may dwell in your hearts through faith.
And I pray that you, being rooted and established in
love. (Ephesians 3:16-17 NIV)

Faith gives us the strength to pursue our dreams. Faith
gives us the courage to see past the fears that continue to
hold us back from living our best lives. Faith is the basis
of understanding that all things are possible!

Everything is possible for one who believes.
(Mark 9:23 ESV)

How has your faith blessed you through your struggles?
I personally have placed my faith and hope in our Lord
for as long as I can remember. It was always natural for
me to do this!

How do we help those who have lost their hope and
faith due to continuous hardships? Through prayer and
the sharing of our personal experiences, we can
encourage others to stay strong through God's love.

Since we are called to minister to one another, we have
opportunities every day to lead by example through our
faith. Our patience, kindness, and ministry can and will
help those who struggle to turn to the love of Christ.

*I can do all things through Christ which strengtheneth me.*
*(Philippians 4:13 KJV)*

So in Christ Jesus you are all children of God through faith. (Galatians 3:26 NIV)

*~Your Faith Means Everything~*

# ♥ Faith for the Future ♥

May the God of hope fill you with all joy and peace in believing, so that by the power of the Holy Spirit you may abound in hope. (Romans 15:13 ESV)

Has 2020 created a bit of anxiety in your heart? The unknown can certainly be a bit troublesome for many of us. But the good news is that God is already there with a plan that is always working according to His Will for us. His plan, His purpose, His way, and His actions will always prevail. If you're struggling with constant uncertainty and live with a restless mind and heart, then pray and know that your faith is bigger than your fears!

For this light momentary affliction is preparing for us an eternal weight of glory beyond all comparison, as we look not to the things that are seen but to the things that are unseen. (2 Corinthians 4:17-18 ESV)

*~Faith, Hope and Trust~*

*I can do all things through Christ which strengtheneth me.*
*(Philippians 4:13 KJV)*

# ❤ Humble Yourself Before the Lord ❤

Do nothing from selfish ambition or conceit, but in the humility count others more significant than yourselves. Let each of you look not only to his own interests, but also to the interests of others. (Philippians 2:3-4 ESV)

Humility is defined as freedom from pride and arrogance. It is lowliness of mind and an act of submission.

Take a moment to reflect on a time where you were humbled during a personal or public experience. Or perhaps you have yet to experience the true meaning of what humility can bring to your life. As children of God, how can we truly humble ourselves before our Lord?

Scripture tells us in James 4:6 ESV, "God opposes the proud, but gives grace to the humble." These are powerful words!

Being puffed up with pride doesn't necessarily come from the words we speak, but rather from our lack of kind actions towards our fellow brothers and sisters in Christ.

Beloved, do not imitate evil but imitate good. Whoever does good is from God; whoever does evil has not seen God. (3 John 1:11 ESV)

To humble ourselves is to admit that we are not in control; for all the control is God's and God's alone! We are called to serve Him and to minister to one another as

*I can do all things through Christ which strengtheneth me.*
*(Philippians 4:13 KJV)*

Christ Jesus has ministered to those needing to be saved. Therefore, let us go forth and exercise our humility before all mankind with full understanding that we do it for our Father in Heaven.

*~No Garment is More Becoming to a Child of God than the Cloak of Humility~*

# ♥What Gets You Through Your Days♥

The steadfast love of the Lord never ceases; his mercies never come to an end; they are new every morning; great is your faithfulness. (Lamentations 3:22-23 ESV)

What gets me through my days is praying, keeping Jesus as my center, exercising, remembering that God is in control, writing on His behalf, taking care of my family and home, helping others where I can, staying busy with kid activities and cleaning, and praying some more. What helps you get through your days? Each new day is a gift, so we must be mindful to give thanks even through our struggles!

So we do not lose heart. Though our outer self is wasting away, our inner self in being renewed day by day. (2 Corinthians 4:16 ESV)

*~Jesus Helps Us All~*

*I can do all things through Christ which strengtheneth me.*
*(Philippians 4:13 KJV)*

# ❤*A Truth*❤

I used to want what others had. I wanted a better marriage to someone else, nicer cars, clothes, and others' freedom to go out and enjoy life. I looked at what appeared to be happy couples in love, and I wanted that.

But by wanting possessions and "stuff", I was severely unhappy and living in a constant state of misery. It wasn't until I really started praying and reading scripture that I fully understood that "stuff" meant nothing in the bigger picture. All that we have will be lost in the end. I learned that I needed to replace my need for wanting things with Jesus.

We are called to not confirm to this world and for good reason. The things in our world are temporary and gone in the blink of an eye. But what lasts forever are our souls. Our souls are precious to Him, and how we live determines where our souls will end up when our possessions are a mere memory.

It's time to wake up and feed our souls with the Word of God! We need to feed our souls with the Gospels of Christ! We need to feed our souls with the truth. The devil had his hand on me long ago and tried pull me down in this world of "want".

But wants and needs do not mean the same to our Father. We simply want things in life, but what we receive are the needs He deems fit for us to have. It has

*I can do all things through Christ which strengtheneth me.*
*(Philippians 4:13 KJV)*

always been His way, and it will continue to only be His way, and this is the best news!

Do not be conformed to this world, but be transformed by the renewal of your mind, that by testing you may discern what is the will of God, what is good and acceptable and perfect. (Romans 12:2 ESV)

*~Do Not Conform~*

# ♥ Jesus Is Always Calling Us ♥

And after you have suffered a little while, the God of all grace, who has called you to his eternal glory in Christ, will himself restore, confirm, strengthen, and establish you. (1 Peter 5:10 ESV)

There will be opportunities every single day where you will be called by our Lord to fulfill your purpose. We hear Him when we slow down, quiet our minds, and open our hearts.

When you seek the Lord with pure intentions, you will experience tears of pure joy. It's like nothing you've ever felt!

Who saved us and called us to a holy calling, not because of our works but because of his own purpose and grace, which he gave us in Christ Jesus before the ages began. (2 Timothy 1:9 ESV)

*~When He Calls You, Will You Answer?~*

*I can do all things through Christ which strengtheneth me.*
*(Philippians 4:13 KJV)*

## ♥ Repentance is a Gift ♥

Repent and turn to Jesus. It's the best decision you'll ever make. Repentance is a freeing choice that takes our sinful pain and turns it into extreme peace of mind! It's letting go our burdens and releasing them to the one who loves us most.

I went into reflective prayer this summer and vocally admitted my sins to God, which resulted in a burning sensation surrounding my throat. I immediately knew that these sins needed to be released, and that the fire I felt rising up were my sins being removed from my soul. This is the first time I have spoken on my experience other than to my daughter.

You see, God already knows our sins. He knows what lays on our hearts, and He understands the confusion that we live with that torments our souls. Let go of the sin!

If we confess our sins, he is faithful and just and will forgive us our sins and purify is from all unrighteousness. (1 John 1:9 NIV)

*~Free Yourself~*

*I can do all things through Christ which strengtheneth me.*
*(Philippians 4:13 KJV)*

# ❤ *Letting Go Feels So Good* ❤

And be not conformed to this world: but be ye transformed by the renewing of your mind, that ye may prove what is that good, and acceptable, and perfect, will of God. (Romans 12:2 KJV)

Has God put something on your heart that you need to let go of? For me, Halloween is no longer an event that I partake in. When I asked God through prayers last year if Halloween is okay to celebrate, His immediate answer was no. I felt it and I had already been questioning it for years. Then came several Biblical signs from strangers and articles that presented themselves to me.

When Fall came this year, I wasn't sure how I'd feel or if I'd miss Halloween; but God is good and I don't miss it one little bit. I feel more awake now than I ever have before! Many friends and family do not understand, but that's okay with me. I care about what God thinks of me. Letting go of earthly things is liberating. If God is putting something on your heart, please listen. He ultimately knows what's best for our souls.

*~Let Go and Renew Your Minds~*

*I can do all things through Christ which strengtheneth me.*
*(Philippians 4:13 KJV)*

## ❤ *He Stands with You Always* ❤

And so we know and rely on the love God has for us.
God is love. Whoever lives in love lives in God, and
God in them. (1 John 4:16 NIV)

Don't be deceived into believing that God doesn't love
you. We all make mistakes, but His love is for everyone.
If you're sinning continually, then it's time to stop. If
you're living a life according to your desires and not
God's Will, then it's time to repent.

Turning to Him is a blessing that we receive time and
time again without fail! He is our strength, our power,
and our salvation. Be strong in God in all of your
struggles! Love Him as much as He loves you.

*~You Can Live a Life of Promise, Joy, and Strength with*
*God on your Side~*

## ❤ *What If You Knew* ❤

For to this you have been called, because Christ also
suffered for you, leaving you an example, so that you
might follow in his steps. (1 Peter 2:21 ESV)

What if you knew your loved ones were not walking
toward Jesus? What if you knew friends who had no
idea how they can be saved? What if you knew that your
example helps them to see God? What if Jesus needs
you to guide them to Him?

*I can do all things through Christ which strengtheneth me.*
*(Philippians 4:13 KJV)*

When you sit and think about how wonderful it is to have Jesus in your life, do you consider sharing this good news with other people?

Rather, speaking the truth in love, we are to grow up in every way into him who is the head, into Christ. (Ephesians 4:15 ESV)

*~This Road Leads to Your Salvation~*

# ❤*Your Heart Is a Gateway to Greatness*❤

And your ears shall hear a word behind you, saying, "This is the way, walk in it", when you turn to the right or when you turn to the left. (Isaiah 30:21 ESV)

Anyone can read the Bible, pray, and be a good person. What helps us to hear our purpose from God, is opening our heart to Him. When we yearn to please God, we are more susceptible to hearing His call for us. It is wonderful news that we are to slow down and listen to His Word!

When the spirit of truth comes, he will guide you into all the truth. (John 16:13 ESV)

*~Greatness Comes by Listening to our Lord~*

*I can do all things through Christ which strengtheneth me.*
*(Philippians 4:13 KJV)*

# ❤️ Faith will Overpower the Darkness ❤️

But they who wait for the Lord shall renew their strength; they shall mount up with wings like eagles; shall run and not be weary; shall walk and not faint.
(Isaiah 40:31 ESV)

This is all about mindset! How do we react when something negative happens in our lives?

Step 1: Pray
Step 2: Breathe and Relax
Step 3: Don't overreact or blame other people
Step 4: Write out pro's & con's
Step 5: Keep your faith
Step 6: Pray again
Step 7: Keep working, keep being a parent, spouse, friend,
   significant other, or coworker
Step 8: Remember that God is bigger than your struggles
Step 9: Count your blessings!
Step 10: Continue to be the good person God made you and allow Him to do the rest.

*~It's Rather Easy to Shine in the Light,*
*but to Glow in the Dark is Mastery~*

*I can do all things through Christ which strengtheneth me.*
*(Philippians 4:13 KJV)*

# ♥ Be Bold, Be Brave, Be a Child of God ♥

Cast not away therefore your confidence, which hath great recompence of reward. (Hebrews 10:35 KJV)

I tend to sit, overthink, complain about my mundane days, and think of something better. In this time, I also feel comfortable, I pray and give thanks, take care of my family, and write. I often think about doing something bold, then I get scared and back down. Have you done this?

But great are the plans that our Lord has for us! Are we willing and able to rise to the occasion? Our answer should immediately be yes! We have all the confidence and courage we need with God by our side.

I've recently decided to take that courage, go out of my comfort zone, and be bold! Since I made this decision, I'm smiling more, I'm more upbeat, and I'm filled with excitement!

Everyone deserves to feel this way. These are the positive emotions that God brings to us when we listen to His plans and purpose for our lives.

If God has placed something on your heart to do, *something positive*, then be brave, be bold, and be a child of God.

*~He Will Only Ever Bring Out the Best in Us~*

*I can do all things through Christ which strengtheneth me.*
*(Philippians 4:13 KJV)*

# ♥ Let Go of the Control ♥

Behold I am the Lord, the God of all flesh. Is anything too hard for me? (Jeremiah 32:27 ESV)

Why is it that we instantly feel we need to be on top of everything we do or be charge of things that consume our energy? We waste so many precious moments from the stress that control causes: wasted moments with our kids and loved ones; and, wasted moments when we should be resting or praying. God literally tells us that He is in complete control. It's actually a gift to us that God is in control and we are not.

So why do bad things happen if God has control? Well, life is hard. It's plain and simple! We will all face trials, but why do we inflict them upon ourselves when we're told to simply trust in God?

Taking on more than you can handle doesn't mean you're an awesome person. It means that you need to learn to settle down and rest. The energizer bunny kept going and going and going, but eventually stopped when the batteries wore out! Our batteries will wear out too.

Having faith in God allows us to understand that we do not have to have it all figured out. We don't have to be on the go one hundred percent of the time. He loves us enough to take on that control we struggle with. Let Him. As long as you're a hard worker and loyal to God, it's okay to give Him the control you can't handle.

*I can do all things through Christ which strengtheneth me.*
*(Philippians 4:13 KJV)*

"There are many devices in a man's heart; nevertheless
the counsel of the Lord, that shall stand."
(Proverbs 19:21 KJV)

*~Be at Peace with Letting Go~*

# ♥ *It's A Perfect Day to Let Go and Let God* ♥

He says, "Be still, and know that I am God; I will be
exalted among the nations, I will be exalted in the
earth." (Psalm 46:10 NIV)

Here we have the perfect reason to be still in our stresses
and to let God do His job. We need to stay consistent in
our faith, humble in our actions, sincere in our prayers,
and trusting in His plan. Let us follow our savior Jesus
Christ in all we do, and continue to work diligently
toward our salvation.

His grace is our grace; go out and spread it! Be
compassionate even toward your enemies, for our
example of Christianity is a forgiving one.

Do not judge according to your dislikes, but rather judge
righteously against sin so that others may see Christ in
your loving example.

*~Be Still Today and Watch God Work~*

*I can do all things through Christ which strengtheneth me.*
*(Philippians 4:13 KJV)*

# ♥ To Be or Not to Be ♥

But the fruit of the Spirit is love, joy, peace,
forbearance, kindness, goodness, faithfulness, gentleness
and self-control. Against such things there is no law.
(Galatians 5:22-23 NIV)

Joy is a decision. Choosing joy is a sacrifice. Choosing
joy goes much deeper than just having a happy day
because things are going well. Choosing joy is deeply
rooted in our faith, hope, and trust in God. However,
being a negative person who continues to complain is
also a choice!

No one forces us to behave this way, not even our
circumstances. Has anything great happened to you from
your complaining and negative thinking? Or, have you
witnessed blessing upon blessing because you have
chosen to feel joy even in your struggles? The first step
to living a joyous life is to smile more. Watch a funny
movie, visit a friend, read your Bible, or help someone
in need!

What brings me joy is helping others and sharing the
Word of God. Going outside of my own internal
struggles and being there for someone else who's
struggling is life changing for us both. The next time
you find yourself complaining, go into prayer and reach
out to someone in need.

*I can do all things through Christ which strengtheneth me.*
*(Philippians 4:13 KJV)*

Rejoice always, pray continually, give thanks in all circumstances; for this is God's will for you in Christ Jesus. (1 Thessalonians 5:16-18 NIV)

*~Every Day We Make a Choice~*

## ♥ *Prayer for Protection* ♥

For he shall give his angels charge over thee, to keep thee in all thy ways. (Psalm 91:11 KJV)

Dear Heavenly Father,

I pray this day for those struggling with inner demons. Please bless those who live in fear and keep them safe in your arms. Please send your angels to protect your righteous children who wish to serve you according to your purpose. We all long for safety, happiness and to live in good health, God. Help us to grow in your everlasting love, and help us to fulfill our purpose here on earth. Please bless your children with peace, wisdom, and safety. Help to remind us to be in constant prayer to guard us from the schemes of the devil. In Jesus' name I pray, Amen

See, I am sending an angel ahead of you to guard you along the way and to bring you to the place I have prepared. (Exodus 23:20 NIV)

*~In Jesus' Name~*

*I can do all things through Christ which strengtheneth me.*
*(Philippians 4:13 KJV)*

# ♥You are a Wonderful Child of God♥

See what kind of love the Father has given to us, that we
should be called children of God; and so we are.
(1 John 3:1 ESV)

You are loved beyond all measure. Receive it, feel it,
and believe in it. God, our Father, does not pick and
choose whom He shall love. He loves and lives for all of
His children, and this means you!

Behold, what manner of love the Father hath bestowed
upon us, that we should be called the sons of God:
therefore the world knoweth us not, because it
knew him not. (1 John 3:1 KJV)

God has made us each unique with the capabilities to
love, to forgive, and to show kindness, peace, patience,
and goodness to all we meet. Keep God and His
commandments close to your heart and flourish in the
love He has for you.

*~You Are His~*

*I can do all things through Christ which strengtheneth me.*
*(Philippians 4:13 KJV)*

# ❤*Don't Be Scared*❤

For I know the thoughts that I think toward you, saith
the Lord, thoughts of peace, and not of evil, to give you
an expected end. (Jeremiah 29:11 KJV)

Many times in our lives, we will come to a crossroad
where we need to choose a direction. Right, left,
straight, or go back from where we came. None of these
paths are typically easy to follow without feeling a sense
of fear and panic. I have yet to meet a person who is
unafraid of the unknown!

What if I were to tell you that you are never alone in
your choices? Did you know that our Lord is with you in
every decision you make? When you feel a sense of
right and wrong, that's Him. He is the Holy Spirit giving
you the strength to pursue the goodness you seek. He's
the driving force that tells you to love, to be kind, to
forgive, and to stand firm in your faith.

*~God Won't Steer You Wrong, Only the Devil Will~*

*I can do all things through Christ which strengtheneth me.*
*(Philippians 4:13 KJV)*

# ♥ *Let Us Give Thanks and Praise* ♥

Give thanks in all circumstances; for this is the will of God in Christ Jesus for you. (1 Thessalonians 5:18 ESV)

I have noticed a monumental difference in my emotions and actions when I choose to be grateful instead of complaining. Complaining brings negative emotions to your spirit, not to mention it alienates you from those you love. You are missing out on the joys in life when you become comfortable in your own state of misery. Our time is precious, and we are meant to live it basking in the glory of God!

Let no corrupting talk come out of your mouths, but only such as is good for building up, as fits the occasion, that it may give grace to those who hear.
(Ephesians 4:29 ESV)

Take your complaints and turn them into prayer. Then in prayer give thanks for your blessings.

*~Christ Jesus Is For You~*

*I can do all things through Christ which strengtheneth me.*
*(Philippians 4:13 KJV)*

# ♥ Have You Ever ♥

Let not mercy and truth forsake thee: bind them about
thy neck; write them upon the tablet of thine heart.
(Proverbs 3:3 KJV)

Have you ever thought that it might be easier to just give
up on your faith? I understand that when times become
challenging, we have unanswered questions and grow
weary in our strength. But even through our struggles,
our faith does not leave us; we are the ones who
abandon our faith. The difference is monumental!

Our Lord's mercy, truth, and love will live on forever,
but our free will stands in our way. It is easy to have
faith when things seem to be going great in our lives! It
is just as easy to let our faith go when hardships fall on
us. We have a God who promises to never leave us nor
forsake us.

It is the Lord who goes before you. He will be with you;
He will not leave you or forsake you. Do not fear or be
dismayed. (Deuteronomy 31:8 ESV)

Go out today, in the midst of your struggles and
thanksgivings, wearing the full armor of our Lord. Stand
firm in your faith against the schemes of the devil and
embrace our Lord.

*~He Is With You Always~*

*I can do all things through Christ which strengtheneth me.*
*(Philippians 4:13 KJV)*

# ♥Grace and Knowledge of Our Lord♥

But grow in grace, and in the knowledge of our Lord and Saviour Jesus Christ. To him be glory both now and forever. Amen (2 Peter 3:18 KJV)

Let us awake to the beauty of our Lord Christ Jesus. When we wake, His glory and mercies are new every day! My prayer for you today is that you wake with a fresh renewal of your heart, mind, and spirit. Look unto the goodness that He brings to your days through prayer and constant communication. Let us grow in grace and knowledge so that we may lead and serve as His true disciples.

*~To Him be Glory Both Now and Forever~*

# ♥Jesus Is Peace♥

And let the peace of God rule in your hearts, to which also ye are called in one body; and be ye thankful.
(Colossians 3:15 KJV)

Let the peace of God rule your hearts, because the peace that He brings is unmeasurable and irreplaceable. In prayer, let your worries, anxieties, and thanksgivings be known to our Lord. When my heart is troubled, I turn to the Him. As my center, He calms my mind and brings peace to my troubled heart. He can do this for you.

*I can do all things through Christ which strengtheneth me.*
*(Philippians 4:13 KJV)*

Peace I leave with you; my peace I give to you. Not as the world gives do I give to you. Let not your hearts be troubled, neither let them be afraid.
(John 14:27 ESV)

*~Freedom and Peace in Jesus is Yours~*

# ♥ It Is Time to Awaken ♥

But stay awake at all times, praying that you may have strength to escape all these things that are going to take place, and to stand before the Son of Man.
(Luke 21:36 ESV)

Dear Heavenly Father,

I pray this day for those who succumb to the grip of Satan. I pray for the lost souls who continue to turn to evil and not to your Holy Word. The time is near when we will face our transgressions and answer for our sins. Please help everyone feel the Holy Spirit and act justly in your sight. The day is drawing near when we will face the Son of Man. Help us to repent of our sins and turn to your light. Amen

Besides this you know the time, that the hour has come for you to wake from sleep. For salvation is nearer to us now than we first believed. (Romans 13:11 ESV)

*~Let Us Share Jesus with the World~*

*I can do all things through Christ which strengtheneth me.*
*(Philippians 4:13 KJV)*

## ♥ Find Strength in Our Lord ♥

He gives strength to the weary and increases the power
of the weak. Even youths grow tired and weary, and
young men stumble and fall; but those who hope in the
Lord will renew their strength. They will soar on wings
like eagles; they will run and not grow weary, they will
walk and not be faint. (Isaiah 40:29-31 NIV)

When you think of all the times that you felt exhausted
and felt that you couldn't go any further, how did you
find the strength to keep moving forward? I have been
tried and tested and exhausted, but each time I went
straight into prayer.

Through God, we find strength! Through Him, we have
hope! We trust in His timing and plan for our lives. On
our personal journeys, we use His Word to heal our
souls and to pray for those who have lost their faith.

If you're feeling defeated, turn to our Lord. If you need
courage and strength, seek answers from our Lord. If
you need love, the Lord our God will bless you.

*~He Gives Strength to the Weary~*

*I can do all things through Christ which strengtheneth me.*
*(Philippians 4:13 KJV)*

# ♥ Roads ♥

In all your ways acknowledge him, and he will make straight your paths. (Proverbs 3:6 ESV)

What seem to be ordinary, mundane days can easily become exciting when you keep your focus on your blessings. They are gifts that free us from feeling despair! His Word provides light in front of each step we take, while providing the direction we so long to seek.

In the movie, *The Wizard of Oz*, Dorothy is instructed to follow the yellow brick road to get her to the emerald city. This is where she finds her way home. It's a journey that brings hardships and scary moments, but it's also a journey that brings new friendships and hope! This is how our journeys will be on the yellow brick roads we choose to take.

So, when you slow down to think about the road you're traveling on, are you taking Jesus with you? We have so many paths and roads we can choose, so just remember that He is walking with you always.

*~Follow Your Yellow Brick Road~*

*I can do all things through Christ which strengtheneth me.*
*(Philippians 4:13 KJV)*

# ♥*Stop, Look and Listen*♥

"Stop, look and listen" is a common phrase we teach young children to do before crossing a street. This allows them to cross safely to the other side. But as adults, how are we proceeding to the other side?

"Stop, look and listen" can also apply to our Spiritual lives! As I walk in the mornings, my mind wonders into prayer and into thinking of others. In your busy lives, do you ever do this?

First, take a moment to stop! Then look around you at all of God's creation. Close your eyes and listen. When we calm our bodies and minds, we are more susceptible to hearing God's Word. In this busy world, it is imperative to slow down and acknowledge His presence. It's okay to slow down! It's okay to pause and look around you to pray and give thanks! It's okay to listen for His gentle voice.

And he said to them, "Pay attention to what you hear: with the measure you use, it will be measured to you, and still more will be added to you." (Mark 4:24 ESV)

*~It's Okay to Slow Down~*

*I can do all things through Christ which strengtheneth me.*
*(Philippians 4:13 KJV)*

# ❤ Inspire Your Family ❤

I am the light of the world. Whoever follows me will not
walk in darkness, but will have the light of life.
(John 8:12 ESV)

We are all familiar with the phrase, "Do as I say, not as I
do". What if we led by a positive, Spiritual example and
lived as "Hear what I say and do as I do"? When taking
up our crosses and following Christ, we are leading
others from darkness to His light.

You see, when we choose to follow Jesus, things here on
earth take a back seat. Our struggles are easily overcome
with Him as our center. He is our constant reminder of
hope, life, love, and light! Our darkness can simply be
washed away by our faith.

"But as for me and my house, we will serve the Lord."
(Joshua 24:15 KJV)

*~Jesus Loves Your Family~*

*I can do all things through Christ which strengtheneth me.*
*(Philippians 4:13 KJV)*

# ♥ *In* ♥

In God, I place my Hope!
In God, I place my Trust!
In God, I place my Fears!
In God, I place my Anxiety!
In God, I place my Worries!
In God, I place the Unknown!
In God, I place my Love!
In God, I place my Loyalty!
In God, I place my Uncertainty!
In God, I place my Soul!

Trust IN the Lord with all your heart, and lean not on your own understanding. (Proverbs 3:5 NIV)

Delight yourself IN the Lord, and he will give you the desires of your heart. (Psalm 37:4 ESV)

IN all your ways acknowledge him, and he will make straight your paths. (Proverbs 3:6 ESV)

The Lord is my strength and my shield; IN him my heart trusts, and I am helped. (Psalm 28:7 ESV)

*~Place All of Your "Ins" In Our Lord~*

*I can do all things through Christ which strengtheneth me.*
*(Philippians 4:13 KJV)*

## ❤ The Prince of Peace ❤

Peace I leave with you; my peace I give to you. Not as
the world gives do I give to you. Let not your hearts be
troubled, neither let them not be afraid.
(John 14:27 ESV)

Why does it always seem easier to focus on the
negatives than on the positives? I feel that people thrive
from the drama that negative situations bring.
Gossiping, venting, giving dramatic opinions, and acting
out of frustration seem to always create a false positive
form of attention. But when we turn our focus to Jesus
during these times of frustration, our mindset can change
in an instant. He is called The Prince of Peace for a
reason. Instead of complaining about the negative things
going on in your life, focus on your blessings!

For to us a child is born, to us a son is given; and the
government shall be upon his shoulder, and his name
shall be called Wonderful Counselor, Mighty God,
Everlasting Father, Prince of Peace. (Isaiah 9:6 ESV)

*~Why Harp on the Negatives when You Can Be Proud of*
*Your Positives~*

*I can do all things through Christ which strengtheneth me.*
*(Philippians 4:13 KJV)*

# ♥ *It's In You* ♥

If we live in the Spirit; let us also walk in the Spirit.
(Galatians 5:25 KJV)

It's a true blessing to recognize that the Spirit of God is within us. Some feel it and some choose to push it aside, but this doesn't mean that God abandons us when we choose to not listen.

The Spirit of God is righteous and true, bearing all good news and deeds needed to be acted out through each of us. Let us all walk as brothers and sisters in Christ through the Spirit that God has called upon us to act.

Who hath saved us, and called us with an holy calling, not according to our works, but according to his own purpose and grace, which was given us in Christ Jesus before the world began (2 Timothy 1:9 KJV)

*~Walk in the Spirit~*

*I can do all things through Christ which strengtheneth me.*
*(Philippians 4:13 KJV)*

# ❤ *It's a Good Day to have a Good Day* ❤

This is the day that the Lord has made; let us rejoice and
be glad in it. (Psalm 118:24 ESV)

I believe that more often than not, we tend to wake up
checking our phones and dreading the day ahead of us. I
too am guilty of this, but what I've learned is that each
new day is a gift!

Time and time again we are given an opportunity to give
God thanks for new chances to do His Will. Take this
day that our Lord has blessed you with and do
something amazing.

The Lord bless you and keep you; the Lord make his
face to shine upon you and be gracious to you.
(Numbers 6:24-25 ESV)

*~Today is a New Day, New Beginning, New You~*

*I can do all things through Christ which strengtheneth me.*
*(Philippians 4:13 KJV)*

# ♥ It's Breathtakingly Beautiful ♥

So teach us to number our days that we may get a heart
of wisdom. (Psalm 90:12 ESV)

Life will knock you down, but faith with give you the
courage to get back up. Life will give you lemons, but
your faith will turn those lemons into lemonade! Life
will bring joyful moments, and your faith will allow you
to share your joys with those who are struggling! Life
will have boring, mundane moments, but your faith will
help you smile, knowing that Jesus loves you! You will
be tired, stressed, and anxious, but your faith will bring
hope for brighter days! Life will sometimes bring
success, and your faith will open your heart to true
gratitude to our Father who reigns now and forever.

Bless the Lord, O my soul, and forget not all his benefits
(Psalm 103:2 ESV)

*~Life Is Beautiful~*

*I can do all things through Christ which strengtheneth me.*
*(Philippians 4:13 KJV)*

# ♥We Have All We Need♥

His divine power has given us everything we need for a
godly life through our knowledge of him who called us
by his own glory and goodness. (2 Peter 1:3 NIV)

I always tell my kids that we'll make sure they have
everything they need in life, but little of what they want.
I let them know that Jesus loves them, and I teach them
the importance of prayer and kindness. These are things
we all need.

However, our wants are different. I want to be
financially secure, but I need Jesus in my life. I want my
children to always be healthy, happy, and safe, but I
need to trust in God to ensure this. I want to help people,
but I need to pray for those I cannot help. I want to be
successful in everything I do, but I need to use the gifts
God gave me.

Don't let your wants outweigh your needs! These are
two very different concepts. God has already instilled in
you what you need in order to live a life of
righteousness.

*~Jesus Fulfills Every Need~*

*I can do all things through Christ which strengtheneth me.*
*(Philippians 4:13 KJV)*

# ♥The Word of the Lord Remains Forever♥

For all flesh is as grass, and all the glory of man as the flower of grass. The grass withereth, and the flower thereof falleth away. (1 Peter 1:24 KJV)

It is no secret that we will wither away at the end of our lives. But even after we've gone, God's Word will remain the same. Our lives are shaped by the knowledge of the Bible. We have a choice to live by it or go against it. This is the free will that has been given to us! His Word, however, is powerful and full of promises and hope.

And this word is the good news that was preached to you. (1 Peter 1:25 ESV)

*~God's Word Is a Promise that Leads to a Fulfilling Life~*

# ♥Humility Is Key♥

With all humility and gentleness, with patience, bearing with one another in love. (Ephesians 4:2 ESV)

The meaning of life is quite simple, yet so many people search a lifetime for it. With houses and cars and wealth, it's what lies in our hearts that will be seen by God. Living a humble lifestyle is giving and not gloating.

One gives freely, yet grows all the richer; another withholds what he should give, and only suffers want

*I can do all things through Christ which strengtheneth me.*
*(Philippians 4:13 KJV)*

. Whoever brings blessing will be enriched, and one who
waters will himself be watered.
(Proverbs 11:24-25 ESV)

Life is beautiful; life is a gift! What we do with our time
will answer the questions we seek about our purpose.
Giving, loving, and sharing; being humble, kind, patient,
and forgiving—these are formidable qualities we are
called to live by.

*~Minister to One Another in Truth and Love~*

# ❤ *Faith, Hope, Love* ❤

And now these three remain: faith, hope and love. But
the greatest of these is love. (1 Corinthians 13:13 NIV)

Love in Corinthians is also known as charity in the King
James Version.

And now abideth faith, hope, charity, these three; but the
greatest of these is charity. (1 Corinthians 13:13 KJV)

Charity is love! It's giving and providing for those who
cannot provide for themselves.

We are called to have faith in things unseen, hope in
Jesus Christ, and charity/love for those in need of
support and prayer.

*~Let Us All Serve One Another In Love~*

*I can do all things through Christ which strengtheneth me.*
*(Philippians 4:13 KJV)*

# ❤Your Pain Will Show Your Purpose❤

The Lord will fulfill his purpose for me; your steadfast
love, O Lord, endures forever. Do not forsake the work
of your hands. (Psalm 138:8 ESV)

The "pit" is a dark place indeed. Sometimes in life, we
go through extremely dark struggles to learn important
lessons. I, for one, would never know the true
understanding of gratitude if my life remained perfect
every single day. It's the struggle that enhances our
blessings.

When we recover from these dark times, we often
wonder why they happened at all. We have questions,
concerns, and sometimes, bitterness. But there will come
a day when our experiences will help someone else who
is battling the same struggles. Do not be afraid to share
your stories! The plans that God has for us may never
make sense, but these plans will save others from their
despair.

For I know the plans I have for you, declares the Lord,
plans for welfare and not for evil, to give you a future
and a hope. (Jeremiah 29:11 ESV)

*~Use Your Experience to Help Others in Need~*

*I can do all things through Christ which strengtheneth me.*
*(Philippians 4:13 KJV)*

# ♥ Don't Be Weighed Down ♥

Give, and it will be given to you. Good measure, pressed down, shaken together, running over, will be put into your lap. For with the measure you use it will be measured back to you. (Luke 6:38 ESV)

I'm happiest when I'm helping others. By helping others, I'm actually fixing my own problems.

Placing your focus on doing good takes away the struggles weighing you down. So, what is it about helping those in need that makes us feel so good?

It's knowing that we're going outside of our own needs to provide encouragement and love for people who have lost hope. We are not called to command others, we are called to serve.

As each has received a gift, use it to serve one another, as good stewards of God's varied grace.
(1 Peter 4:10 ESV)

*~Serve One Another in the Name of Jesus Christ~*

*I can do all things through Christ which strengtheneth me.*
*(Philippians 4:13 KJV)*

# ♥God Loves You♥

So we have come to know and to believe the love that
God has for us. God is love, and whoever abides in love
abides in God, and God abides in him.
(1 John 4:16 ESV)

Dear Heavenly Father,

I pray this day for those who feel abandoned or lost, and
for those who are filled with despair. I pray that they
feel the power of the Holy Spirit helping them turn to
you in these difficult times. May your arms of eternal
love wrap around them like a mother comforting her
sick child. So many people need to know you love them
every single day, because it's your love alone that
carries them through their struggles. Thank you for
loving us, and please continue to help us feel your
never-ending presence. Amen

Fear not, for I am with you: be not dismayed, for I am
your God; I will strengthen you, I will help you, I will
uphold you with my righteous right hand.
(Isaiah 41:10 ESV)

*~God Loves You More than Anything~*

*I can do all things through Christ which strengtheneth me.*
*(Philippians 4:13 KJV)*

# ♥Don't Be Afraid, Only Believe♥

Overhearing what they said, Jesus told him, "Don't be afraid; just believe." (Mark 5:36 NIV)

We often go through life filled with the dread of new things approaching. What would a life look like without worry and fear? This is a foreign concept to most people.

A new outlook on life begins with faith! Faith is the belief and trust in God. Our fears and worries start to diminish when we focus purely on our faith in His Holy Word. "Don't be afraid; only believe" should mark the promise of new beginnings on your journey.

So faith comes from hearing, and hearing through the word of Christ. (Romans 10:17 ESV)

*~Just Believe~*

*I can do all things through Christ which strengtheneth me.*
*(Philippians 4:13 KJV)*

# ♥Adjust Your Attitude♥

Do all things without grumbling or disputing, that you may be blameless and innocent, children of God without blemish in the midst of a crooked and twisted generation, among whom you shine as lights in the world. (Philippians 2:14-15 ESV)

Our attitudes determine our reaction to stressful situations. When confronted with difficult people, it's okay to step back, take a breath, and think before you respond. All stressful encounters can be positively conquered by remembering that God is with you. When we wear the full armor of our Lord, we become brave, righteous, and unstoppable. This also comes with the ability to remain calm and level headed.

Finally, be strong in the Lord and in the strength of his might. (Ephesians 6:10 ESV)

*~Most of your Stress Comes from the Way You Respond, Not the Way Life Is~*

*I can do all things through Christ which strengtheneth me.*
*(Philippians 4:13 KJV)*

# ♥ Character Is Key ♥

Whoever walks in integrity walks securely, but he who
makes his ways crooked will be found out.
(Proverbs 10:9 ESV)

Jesus walked with integrity, which seems to a rare trait
in people today. Those who choose to be strong in their
character typically walk alone. We grow spiritually
when we choose to make kind choices out of love for
others.

Our walk as brothers and sisters in Christ will be
difficult. It may come with ridicule, and more often than
not, we will find that we lose friends along the way. But
our character and ethical standards will take us further in
life than how we respond to the status of our reputations.

Always worry about your character and not your
reputation, because your character is who you are, and
your reputation is only what people think of you.

*~Walk with Character, Not by the Opinion of Others~*

*I can do all things through Christ which strengtheneth me.*
*(Philippians 4:13 KJV)*

# ♥Even On Days When It Is Hard♥

Bearing with one another and, if one has a complaint
against another, forgiving each other; as the Lord has
forgiven you, so you also must forgive.
(Colossians 3:13 ESV)

I know you're struggling with forgiving those who have
wronged you and those who have brought pain into your
life. I too have struggled with this. But what is more
difficult to live with is the hate we carry around. This
hate drowns out blessings that we receive and masks our
joy with bitterness. This bitterness trickles into our
family life, work life, and personal life. The stress is too
much to bear!

I've learned that through prayer and trust in the Lord's
plan, I'm able to forgive and allow God change the
action of those I cannot change. It is also easier to
forgive knowing that God has called us to do so.

Therefore, confess your sins to one another and pray for
one another, that you may be healed. The prayer of a
righteous person has great power as it is working.
(James 5:16 ESV)

*~Pray to Forgive and to be Forgiven~*

*I can do all things through Christ which strengtheneth me.*
*(Philippians 4:13 KJV)*

## ❤ *My Favorite* ❤

Trust in the Lord with all your heart, and do not lean on
your own understanding. (Proverbs 3:5 ESV)

Proverbs 3:5 has changed my life! When I feel
overwhelmed and overly stressed, His Word heals my
soul. It is a reminder that He is in absolute control of
everything in this world.

I do my part by praying, sharing His Word, and being a
good person. But the rest of it that I cannot control, I
leave to him. He is my strength and I place my trust in
Him always.

If you're struggling with anxiety and uncertainty, please
just remember to whom you belong! You are loved and
treasured beyond all measure.

*~Take this Day to Pray and Ask God to Take Away your*
*Anxiety and Worries~*

*I can do all things through Christ which strengtheneth me.*
*(Philippians 4:13 KJV)*

## ♥God is Seen through our Love for all People♥

Beloved, let us love one another, for love is from God, and whoever loves has been born of God and knows God. Anyone who does not love does not know God, because God is love. (1 John 4:7-8 ESV)

Dear God,
Thank you for bringing us here today to read your message on love. We ask that you bless us through the words we are about to read, and we ask that you give us the courage to go out and share your love with everyone we meet, so that through us all people see you. We pray these things in Jesus' name, Amen

We love because he first loved us. If anyone says, "I love God," and hates his brother, he is a liar; for he who does not love his brother whom he has seen cannot love God whom he has not seen. And this commandment we have from him: whoever loves God must also love his brother. (1 John 4:19-21 ESV)

For God so loved the world, that he gave his only Son, that whoever believes in him should not perish but have eternal life. (John 3:16 ESV)

*~Stop Sinning and Start Loving~*

*I can do all things through Christ which strengtheneth me.*
*(Philippians 4:13 KJV)*

# ❤ Keep Fighting through your Battles ❤

But the Lord is with me as a dread warrior; therefore my
persecutors will stumble; they will not overcome me.
They will be greatly shamed, for they will not succeed.
Their eternal dishonor will never be forgotten.
(Jeremiah 20:11 ESV)

Do things come easy in life? No, not usually. Is it worth
fighting for what you believe in? Yes, absolutely!
Things did not come easy for Jesus, but He stood firm in
His faith until the very end. He fought temptations, He
fought against evil-doers, and He fought to save us from
our sins. He did this while preaching the Word of God,
living the Word of God, and living a life without sin.
What a role model!

Growing up, I often heard the phrase, "What would
Jesus do?". As an adult, I just now fully understand the
impactful meaning behind these four small words! Take
some time today to reflect on how you too can be more
like Jesus.

Put on the whole armor of God, that you may be able to
stand against the schemes of the devil.
(Ephesians 6:11 ESV)

*~Warriors Aren't the Ones Who Always Win, But the*
*Ones Who Always Fight~*

*I can do all things through Christ which strengtheneth me.*
*(Philippians 4:13 KJV)*

# ❤*Commandment One*❤

Love the Lord your God with all your heart and with all
your soul and with all your strength.
(Deuteronomy 6:5 NIV)

Are we truly capable of loving God more than ourselves,
our families, and our earthly possessions? The answer is
"Yes"!

He is our Creator, our Father, and our biggest form of
support. His love for us is endless; so, in return, our love
should remain the same toward Him. When you make it
a habit of praying and speaking to Him, you will
understand the importance of having this loving
connection.

How precious is your unfailing love, O God!
(Psalm 36:7 ESV)

*~We are Called to Love God~*

# ❤*Everyday*❤

Then shall ye call upon me, and ye shall go and pray
unto me, and I will harken unto you.
(Jeremiah 29:12 KJV)

Do not ever be afraid of communicating with your
children at any age. And children, do not ever be afraid
to communicate with your parents at any age. Family is
forever, and we are given opportunity after opportunity
to open our hearts to one another. Be truthful, be sincere,

and good and bad. Say I Love You every chance you get! Hug one another in tears of joy and sadness. Be a strong family that communicates and respects one another.

Rejoicing in hope; patient in tribulation; continuing instant in prayer. (Romans 12:12 KJV)

*~Pray and Communicate to Your Kids Everyday~*

# ❤ Freedom Is Ours ❤

Now the Lord is that spirit: and where the spirit of the Lord is, there is liberty. (2 Corinthians 3:17 KJV)

Liberty means freedom! So, imagine what a stress-free life would look like for you. For me, this would mean imagining that my parenting and financial stresses were gone.

Well, when we pray, we are able to release the stresses we bear and feel the freedom that God offers by taking our burdens from us. Prayer is an amazing gift that each and every one of us has been given. Use this gift every chance you get so that you can live in the freedom God gives!

Live as people who are free, not using your freedom as a cover-up for evil, but living as servants of God.
(1 Peter 2:16 ESV)

*~Freedom to Serve~*

*I can do all things through Christ which strengtheneth me.*
*(Philippians 4:13 KJV)*

# ❤*Plant Seeds and Lead by Example*❤

Not neglecting to meet together, as is the habit of some, but encouraging one another, and all the more as you see the Day drawing near. (Hebrews 10:25 ESV)

We are taught through Scripture to love and to pray for one another. We are not to neglect those in need or to ignore those who are inquisitive about Christ. Let us educate and lead by Christ's example to share His love! The way we live as Christians, should prove to the world that we have an awesome God. Don't lose faith, don't lose hope, and don't turn away from Jesus Christ.

That I may know him and the power of his resurrection, and may share his sufferings, and becoming like him in his death. (Philippians 3:10 ESV)

*~Your Life as a Christian Should Make Nonbelievers Question Their Disbelief in God~*

# ❤*Stay Strong*❤

I can do all things through Christ which strengtheneth me. (Philippians 4:13 KJV)

Take a few moments to imagine the events that took place on the day of Christ's crucifixion. Think about what He went through and imagine the love He must have felt for us. This was the ultimate sacrifice!

*I can do all things through Christ which strengtheneth me.*
*(Philippians 4:13 KJV)*

Who wouldn't lay their own life down for their children and loved ones? I would, you would, and Jesus did. We are here because of His sacrifice, and that is the greatest love I've ever known.

So, when you're struggling in this life, just remember that Jesus Christ died for your sins, and you can do anything through the strength of His love for you.

*~Jesus Loved You Then, He Loves You Now, He'll Love You Forever~*

## ♥ God Is Love ♥

And we have known and believed the love that God hath for us. God is love; and he that dwelleth in love dwelleth in God, and God in him. (1 John 4:16 KJV)

Dear Heavenly Father,

I pray this morning for those living with a troubled heart. I pray they learn that your love for them brings hope and brighter days ahead. Please help us to share your love with those who live with hardened hearts. Please help to show them patience, kindness, and compassion as Jesus has shown to us. These things I pray in your Son's Holy name. Amen

*~God is Real, God is Love and God is for You~*

*I can do all things through Christ which strengtheneth me.*
*(Philippians 4:13 KJV)*

# ♥ Just Do It ♥

It is no surprise that life will be tough sometimes. But I am actually surprised when good things happen! Why is this? When we trust and keep God as our center, shouldn't we be knowledgeable that we are blessed even in the midst of our struggles?

I have been crucified with Christ. It is no longer I who live, but Christ who lives in me. And the life I now live in the flesh I live by faith in the Son of God, who loved me and gave himself for me. (Galatians 2:20 ESV)

We have two choices in life. We either give up when life throws lemons at us, or we stand firm in our faith and push through while keeping Jesus as our center. We Just Do It!

The Devil has one mission and that is to control you. God's mission is to love you! So, when we give up, the devil wins. When we push through, God's love and strength is with us.

But by pushing through, be sure you're not hurting other people in the process. We are all brothers and sisters in Christ trying to live the best life we can. So, stay strong in Christ, push through your struggles, and just do it! Just do it—quietly and unobtrusively. That is the way your God, who conceived you in love, working behind the scenes, helps you out.

*~Don't Give Up~*

*I can do all things through Christ which strengtheneth me.*
*(Philippians 4:13 KJV)*

## ❤ This Is Why ❤

Finally, be strong in the Lord and in the strength of his might. Put on the whole armor of God, that you may be able to stand against the schemes of the devil.
(Ephesians 6:10-11 ESV)

We are called to minister to one another! As humans, we have the tendency to lose hope, lose faith, and give up. This is not what our Lord wants from us!

We are to constantly wear the armor of God and face our challenges head on with His Protection. We are called to share His Word and to help one another as brothers and sisters in Christ.

Think for a moment about David facing Goliath. King Saul had ordered David to wear his battle armor. Uncomfortable and large on David, he refused and knew that He was protected by God's armor alone. He faced Goliath head on and beat him in the name of the Lord. We, too, are called to be like David.

*~Put on the Armor of God and Help Those Who Have Lost Hope~*

*I can do all things through Christ which strengtheneth me.*
*(Philippians 4:13 KJV)*

# ♥Struggles Shouldn't Define Relationships♥

Therefore a man shall leave his father and his mother and hold fast to his wife, and they shall become one flesh. (Genesis 2:24 ESV)

Marriage is a beautiful journey! Understandably there will be stressful moments of parenting—lack of communication, finances, work, and time together—but praying for your spouse is a gift. When the communication lines are open and you start working together as one flesh, as a team, then great things will happen in your union. Pray for one another, talk through your stressful moments, hug every single day, and make time for one another. Do not get lost in the business of parenting and working. Get lost in the love you have for one another and everything else will fall into place.

Love is patient and kind; love does not envy or boast; it is not arrogant or rude. It does not insist on its own way; it is not irritable or resentful; it does not rejoice at wrongdoing, but rejoices with the truth. Love bears all things, believes all things, hopes all things, endures all things. (1 Corinthians 13:4-7 ESV)

*~Overcome your Relationship Struggles Together~*

# ❤ *Love and Hate Do Not Go Hand in Hand* ❤

If a man say, I love God, and hateth his brother, he is a liar: for he that loveth not his brother whom he hath seen, how can he love God whom he hath not seen? (1 John 4:20 KJV)

I'm noticing that it is becoming seemingly easier in our world to criticize and hate those who we do not see eye to eye with. Not everyone agreed with Jesus, yet He loved them.

A new commandment I give unto you, That ye love one another; as I have loved you, that ye also love one another. (John 13:34 KJV)

Be aware of the devil and the sneaky ways he uses to turn us against one another! Hate and deception are Satan's playground. Love and peace are the root of Jesus' being. See the difference?

O you who love the LORD, hate evil! He preserves the lives of his saints; he delivers them from the hand of the wicked. (Psalm 97:10 ESV)

*~We Cannot Pray in Love yet Live in Hate~*

*I can do all things through Christ which strengtheneth me.*
*(Philippians 4:13 KJV)*

# ❤ *God is Bigger than Your Struggles* ❤

The Lord is my rock, my fortress and my deliverer; my
God is my rock, in whom I take refuge, my shield and
the horn of my salvation, my stronghold.
(Psalm 18:2 NIV)

I struggle, you struggle, we all struggle! And this is okay
when we face challenges in life. What we all must
remember is that our Lord is here watching over us.
He's our biggest cheerleader in life!

If you are continually feeling down and out, look up and
grow in prayer, and trust in God. Take a step back, take
a deep breath, and let your anxieties go in prayer.

*~He's Our Constant Rock and Fortress~*

# ❤ *Living Water* ❤

He that believeth on me, as the scripture hath said, out of
his belly shall flow rivers of living water.
(John 7:38 KJV)

Living water will flow from you! Peace will overcome
your soul! His Word will protect you as armor would a
knight! Your faith will lead your heart to great success
in the name of our Lord! Your hope will anchor your
soul and see you through to a brighter tomorrow! Do not
give up! Be brave and courageous in the name of Christ

*I can do all things through Christ which strengtheneth me.*
*(Philippians 4:13 KJV)*

Jesus! Prepare yourself before the Lord our God, and stand firm in the faith that has brought you to His glory.

*~His Word is the Water We Drink~*

# ♥ It's All Right Here ♥

The book of law shall not depart from your mouth, but you shall meditate on it day and night, so that you may be careful to do according to all that is written in it. For then you will make your way prosperous, and then you will have good success. (Joshua 1:8 ESV)

All of the answers you're searching for from this moment on are found within the pages of the Holy Bible. From our creation in Genesis in the Old Testament to Revelation in the New Testament, it's all right here. From the beginning until the end there will be laws, wars, freedom, peace, pursuits, commandments, leaders, Kings, followers, betrayals, and heroes. All of which will lead to the coming of Jesus Christ. Every part of the Bible is essential in our pursuit of knowledge and wisdom concerning our own personal survival.

But he answered, "It is written, Man shall not live by bread alone, but by every word that comes from the mouth of God." (Matthew 4:4 ESV)

*~Open Your Bible and Share His Word with Others~*

*I can do all things through Christ which strengtheneth me.*
*(Philippians 4:13 KJV)*

# ❤Let Us Humble Ourselves before Our Lord❤

Humble yourselves, therefore, under the mighty hand of
God so that at the proper time he may exalt you.
(1 Peter 5:6 ESV)

Often times we find it difficult to let go of our pride.
Too much pride can harden our hearts, even against
God. But humility is the condition of being humble;
being modest. Humbling ourselves opens our hearts to
the gift of repentance.

Sharing our sins with God and asking for forgiveness is
something people see as weakness, when in fact, it is a
power we have been given! It is not easy living in a state
of humility. In fact, it is rather difficult and it takes
courage to humble ourselves before God. Use this power
you have been blessed with to repent and to love as
Jesus has loved you.

Humble yourselves in the sight of the Lord, and he shall
lift you up. (James 4:10 KJV)

*~Humility Is Key~*

*I can do all things through Christ which strengtheneth me.*
*(Philippians 4:13 KJV)*

# ♥Clean Cut Scripture♥

The fear of the Lord is the beginning of wisdom, and
knowledge of the Holy One is understanding.
(Proverbs 9:10 NIV)

If you want honest and upfront Scripture, read Proverbs.
It is my favorite! It is clean cut Scripture that tells us
what to do and what not to do. It tells us to trust! It tells
us to turn from evil! It tells us to follow and love God.

When I was a child, I strongly disliked my mother
telling me what to do and giving me endless chores. I
finally just asked her to make me a list of things that
needed to be done, and I would follow her instructions. I
was able follow the chore lists one by one and check
them off as they were completed. This enabled me to
read, understand, and follow. I interpret our Lord's
commands the same way. They are written as
instructions to better our lives!

You see, God isn't here to boss us around like I thought
my mother was doing. He has written these important
things for our benefit, just as I see now that my mother
was doing the same thing.

Responsibility has its rewards. We are called to listen,
retain, and follow, and this is awesome news!

*~Instruction Betters Our Lives~*

*I can do all things through Christ which strengtheneth me.*
*(Philippians 4:13 KJV)*

# ♥ *Positive vs. Pretending* ♥

Now faith is the assurance of things hoped for, the conviction of things not seen. (Hebrews 11:1 ESV)

I don't pretend everything in my life is okay or easy. I vent, I cry, and I pray. What some people see as possible pretend tendencies, is actually me fighting against my demons with a positive mindset. That is due to my strong faith.

Anyone can pretend to have a great life, when behind the scenes there's nothing but darkness. But being positive is what helps you through the dark times. Our faith is the basis of knowing that anything is possible. And when we place our faith in God, we can then understand that negative thinking will lead to unrighteous behavior. Pretending is lying about your circumstances. Staying positive is admitting you struggle, but are choosing to overcome those struggles with faith and trust in God.

Bless the LORD, O my soul, and forget not all his benefits, who forgives all your iniquity, who heals all your diseases, who redeems your life from the pit, who crowns you with steadfast love and mercy.
(Psalm 103:2-4 ESV)

*~Staying Positive will Pay Off in the End~*

*I can do all things through Christ which strengtheneth me.*
*(Philippians 4:13 KJV)*

# ♥Do You Ever♥

Even the Spirit of truth, whom the world cannot receive, because it neither sees him nor knows him, he dwells with you and will be with you. (John 14:17 ESV)

Do you ever feel like there's something important you should be doing? Do you ever feel in your heart that a little something is missing?

I woke up feeling some disconnect this morning. I immediately felt uncertain! After praying and taking a few minutes outside alone to contemplate these feelings, I've now decided to write about it.

People wake up and go to church, or work, or tend to their children and chores, or immediately start exercising. I do not feel the need to tend to any of these this morning, but rather turn straight to God!

You see, when we need guidance, there is only one to whom we can turn to get answers. My heart is beginning to release the negative emotions, and my soul is feeling closer to my Father. I also received an added bonus of contentment when my five-year-old sang "Jesus Loves Me" to make me feel better.

*~Keep Jesus Close~*

*I can do all things through Christ which strengtheneth me.*
*(Philippians 4:13 KJV)*

# ♥ Take Care of Yourself ♥

Beloved, I pray that all may go well with you and that you may be in good health, as it goes well with your soul. (3 John 1:2 ESV)

It is okay to take care of yourself! We can only parent, work, educate, nurture, and help others for so long before our soul burns out. Sleep when you're tired, exercise when your body is unhealthy, pray when your heart is discouraged, and rest your soul in the love of our Father.

Do you not know that you are God's temple and that God's Spirit dwells in you? (1 Corinthians 3:16 ESV)

*~Love Yourself Through Pausing, Praying, Resting, Exercising, and Meditating~*

# ♥ Change Can be a Good Thing ♥

For I know the plans I have for you, declares the Lord, plans for welfare and not for evil, to give you a future and a hope. (Jeremiah 29:11 ESV)

*I can do all things through Christ which strengtheneth me.*
*(Philippians 4:13 KJV)*

Trust in the Lord with all your heart, and do not lean on
your own understanding. In all your ways acknowledge
Him, and He will make straight your path.
(Proverbs 3:5-6 ESV)

These two Scripture passages have changed my life. In
some of my most stressful moments and deepest
struggles, I used these. Not only did I read them, but I
actively applied them to my life.

We can read the Bible and listen to sermons, but it
becomes our job to actively live in His Word! We can
hear His Word, but do we actually listen?

To completely trust God, you must fully understand that
He is in control and recognize that you are not. Next,
you must pray diligently in every situation. This allows
you to rely on His comfort. Finally, you must sit back,
do what you need to do in life, and allow God to work
on your behalf.

Delight yourself in the Lord, and he will give you the
desires of your heart. Commit your way to the Lord;
trust in him, and he will act. He will bring forth your
righteousness as the light, and your justice as the
noonday. (Psalm 37:4-6 ESV)

*~My Life Changed When I Learned to Trust God~*

*I can do all things through Christ which strengtheneth me.*
*(Philippians 4:13 KJV)*

# ♥ Listen Up ♥

The council of the Lord Stands forever, the plans of his
heart to all generations. (Psalm 33:11 ESV)

Don't change the Word of God to fit your comfort level.
His Word is everlasting and unchanging! It is we who
change to conform to our own earthly and humanmade
agendas.

When we fall into the repetition of sinning, it's easy to
say that God will love us anyway. However, there are
stipulations to this. We are called to repent and to take
up our cross and follow Christ. We are not called to sin,
but we are called to love, repent, and sin no more.

Is this easy? Absolutely not! But we have an awesome
God who reigns over the Heavens for eternity. I feel
relieved when I repent! It's a huge release of the burdens
I bear. These are burdens I have created through sin, and
nothing takes the stress away other than prayer and
repentance.

When I sit down to write to you, I reflect on what I need
to say and what I feel people need to hear. It will be bold
and

*I can do all things through Christ which strengtheneth me.*
*(Philippians 4:13 KJV)*

to the point. This is what I prayed to God to have me do for others. I do not believe in sugarcoating His Word. At first, I was afraid and meek, but now I am bold and upfront.

We learn nothing from being comfortable; we learn everything from the Bible's bold messages and parables.

We are led to think, to learn, and to obtain the knowledge through Scripture. Our lives are formed from the messages we receive and how we share them with others. We have a sovereign God who loves us, but it our job to not live by bread alone. We are to live according to His Holy Word.

If you are caught up in judging others with different opinions, stop it and love them. If you are negative and selfish, stop it and start helping others in need. If you have lost faith and hope in our Lord, step up through prayer and education through the Bible.

If you do not agree with this message, take a breath and pray on it. It might be something God needs you to hear and share with others.

*~Be Still and Know that I am God~*

*I can do all things through Christ which strengtheneth me.*
*(Philippians 4:13 KJV)*

## ♥ A Moments Peace ♥

Rejoice in hope, be patient in tribulation, be constant in
prayer. (Romans 12:12 ESV)

If you let every little thing that goes wrong bother you,
you will never know a moments peace. Let go and let
God. When we place our complete trust in God, amazing
things happen to our negative emotions. They disappear.

Have you not known? Have you not heard? The Lord is
the everlasting God, the creator of the ends of the earth.
He does not faint or grow weary; his understanding is
unsearchable. He gives power to the faint, and to him
who has no might he increases strength.
(Isaiah 40:28-29 ESV)

Have I not commanded you? Be strong and courageous.
Do not be frightened, and do not be dismayed, for the
Lord your God is with you wherever you go.
(Joshua 1:9 ESV)

*~Rest Your Mind, Body and Soul~*

## ♥ Let It Go ♥

Cast your burden on the Lord, and he will sustain you;
he will never permit the righteous to be moved.
(Psalm 55:22 ESV)

*I can do all things through Christ which strengtheneth me.*
*(Philippians 4:13 KJV)*

Every single human will feel these negative emotions in life. So, what do we do with them? We let them go and give them to God.I've spent years of my life bitter, angry, and resentful, and trust me, it's no way to find peace. God is gracious, merciful, and forgiving. He has been my rock, my fortress, and my peace! He can be yours too.

Casting all your anxieties on him, because he cares for you. (1 Peter 5:7 ESV)

*~No More Anger, Fear, Sadness, Hate, Regret or Pain~*

## ❤ *Seasons of Change* ❤

I am Alpha and Omega, the beginning and the end, the first and the last. (Revelation 22:13 KJV)

If you haven't already done so, now is the time to dive deep into the study of Revelation. The warnings are clear, and the times are changing! Remember that God loves you, and repentance is a gift not to be feared.

Jesus was sent to save us, and we've been told not to conform to any other ideologies that are manmade.

The Bible is our gift to guide us through these times of change and times of unbelief. Don't stray, don't turn away, and don't give up on your faith.

*~Praise the Lord Jesus Christ~*

*I can do all things through Christ which strengtheneth me.*
*(Philippians 4:13 KJV)*

# ♥Keep Your Eyes on the Lord Always♥

I am the light of the world. (John 8:12 ESV)

Do not allow your minds to be flooded by the news. It's negative, hateful, and full of deception. You get this one life to live to the fullest! Spend your time on following Jesus. This path leads to forgiveness, love, peace, and light!

Our world is full of darkness, but don't let it consume you. Keep your eyes on the Lord, and look to Him always! In every situation, pray and give thanks. Turn from the devil and be saved by Christ.

For while bodily training is of some value, godliness is of value in every way, as it holds promise for the present life and also for the life to come. (1 Timothy 4:8 ESV)

*~Focus on Jesus Always~*

# ♥Dear God♥

Have I not commanded you? Be strong and courageous. Do not be frightened, and do not be dismayed, for the Lord your God is with you wherever you go. (Joshua 1:9 ESV)

Dear God,
If I'm wrong, correct me.
If I am lost, guide me.
If I start to give up, keep me going. Amen

*I can do all things through Christ which strengtheneth me.*
*(Philippians 4:13 KJV)*

This prayer is extremely helpful when faced with the uncertainties of this process called life. I pray that each and everyone one of you knows how beautiful you are inside and out. Let's go out and have a productive day knowing that God is with us! Believe in our Lord and all His ways, for He is good and He is with us in our time of need.

*~God Is Good~*

# ♥ Be A Lion ♥

The wicked flee when no man pursueth: but the righteous are bold as a lion. (Proverbs 28:1 KJV)

More often than not, we allow the fear of another's opinion of us keep us from pursuing the truth. If we see that unrighteous, evil people exist around every corner, why is it difficult for us to act justly against them? We are called to love, but we are also called to share the truth! We are not here to adapt to sin; we are called to show those sinners the light of Jesus Christ.

Everyone who makes practice of sinning also practices lawlessness; sin is lawlessness. (1 John 3:4 ESV)

*~The Righteous are Bold as Lions~*

*I can do all things through Christ which strengtheneth me.*
*(Philippians 4:13 KJV)*

# ❤ *More Glorifying Equals Less Stress* ❤

How much time do you invest in reading your Bible?

This Book of the Law shall not depart from your mouth,
but you shall meditate on it day and night, so that you
may be careful to do according to all that is written in it.
For then you will make your way prosperous, and then
you will have good success. (Joshua 1:8 ESV)

How much time do you invest in talking to Jesus?

Come to me, all who labor and are heavy laden, and I
will give you rest. Take my yoke upon you, and learn
from me, for I am gentle and lowly in heart, and you
will find rest for your souls. For my yoke is easy, and
my burden is light. (Matthew 11:28-30 ESV)

How much time do you devote to glorifying God and
giving thanks and praise?

I will give thanks to you, O Lord my God, with all my
heart, and will glorify your name forever.
(Psalm 86:12 ESV)

Even though I pray and write daily, I could always
spend more time in relationship with Him. We all could.

*~ Every Day is a Beautiful Day to Grow Closer to our
Lord~*

*I can do all things through Christ which strengtheneth me.*
*(Philippians 4:13 KJV)*

# ♥All or Nothing♥

Delight yourself in the Lord, and he will give you the desires of your heart. Commit your way to the Lord; trust in him, and he will act. He will bring forth your righteousness as the light, and your justice as the noonday. (Psalm 37:4-6 ESV)

We either place our full trust in our Lord or we don't. We commit or we don't. We stay loyal or we stray. We believe or we doubt. We accept or we rebuke. We acknowledge Him in all of our ways, or we lead ourselves along a path of unrighteousness. The choice is ours, but I guarantee you'll live a more calm and joyous life by trusting Him.

And if you faithfully obey the voice of the Lord your God, being careful to do all his commandments that I command you today, the Lord your God will set you high above all the nations of the earth. And all these blessings shall come upon you and overtake you, if you obey the voice of the Lord your God. Blessed shall you be in the city, and blessed shall you be in the field. Blessed shall be the fruit of your womb and the fruit of your ground and the fruit of your cattle, the increase of your herds and the young of your flock.
(Deuteronomy 28:1-4 ESV)

*~Trust In the Lord with All Your Heart~*

*I can do all things through Christ which strengtheneth me.*
*(Philippians 4:13 KJV)*

# ❤ No Doubt ❤

Jesus immediately reached out his hand and took hold of him, saying to him, "O you of little faith, why did you doubt?" (Matthew 14:31 ESV)

If we fail, we learn from it. But if we doubt, we become paralyzed from using the ability to succeed in our journeys! You are capable! I am capable! We are all capable! This is the time to throw your doubts out the window and place your trust in God who has created you to be amazing!

Do you not know that you are God's temple and that God's Spirit dwells in you? (1 Corinthians 3:16 ESV)

The Holy Spirit dwells in us to keep us alert, brave, loyal, wise, kind, active, forgiving, loving, and faithful. God has placed us in His hands as a reminder that we belong to Him. With His constant presence, we must not fear. We must not live in a constant state of doubt. Doubt, worry, anxiety, and fear take us further from Him and closer to the one who comes to destroy our souls.

But let him ask in faith, with no doubting, for the one who doubts is like a wave of the sea that is driven and tossed by the wind. (James 1:6 ESV)

*~Stop Doubting and Start Believing~*

*I can do all things through Christ which strengtheneth me.*
*(Philippians 4:13 KJV)*

# ♥ It's Happening More and More ♥

Jesus stood up and said to her, "Woman, where are they? Has no one condemned you?" She said, "No one, Lord." And Jesus said, "Neither do I condemn you; go, and from now on sin no more." (John 8:10-11 ESV)

We've been commanded to not conform to this world, yet every day we are finding ways to conform. Even some churches are changing Scripture to fit a certain agenda created by our society. People are afraid to say no, and some are abandoning their faith out of fear and joining new-age theologies.

The Bible warns us of these events. It is more important now than ever to stand firm in the Gospel of Christ! We are to love and forgive, yet are called to judge righteously against sin and lead people to the Word of God. We are not called to forgive then tell people it's okay to keep sinning. We are to lead as an example of Christ in the way of living a sinless life. It is extremely difficult to do this, but not impossible. For with God all things are possible.

*~Go and Sin No More~*

*I can do all things through Christ which strengtheneth me.*
*(Philippians 4:13 KJV)*

# ❤*Someone Needs You*❤

Let each of you look not only to his own interests, but
also to the interests of others. (Philippians 2:4 ESV)

I truly believe that a big purpose we have is to help
others. It may not be obvious as to what or how we are
to help, but our outreach and sharing in the Word of God
saves lives! We are all called to be disciples in Christ
and to minister to one another.

What does that look like in your life? How can you
minister and help those who are hopeless?

It all starts with the love in your heart and the words in
the Bible. Someone right now needs you and is relying
on an angel for help. If you feel that nudge in your heart,
don't hesitate.

God didn't add another day in your life because you
need it; He added it because someone out there needs
you!

*~Act Today~*

*I can do all things through Christ which strengtheneth me.*
*(Philippians 4:13 KJV)*

# ♥*So Much Is Happening*♥

Therefore be ye also ready: for in such an hour as ye
think not the Son of man cometh.
(Matthew 24:44 KJV)

Matthew 24...take the time to read it!

The evil doers, earthquakes, fires (now overtaking the
Amazon), the rise of Israel, nations against one another,
floods, famine, wars, division amongst God's children,
false prophets and false gods, the sexually immoral,
liars, adulterers, people abandoning their faith, etc.

Jesus has been sent to us so that we can have eternal
salvation. But Jesus is the only way to obtain it. He
came once and He is set to come again! I do not know
when, but things happening in our world match the
warnings in the Bible. This is very serious, and even if
it's not for another one hundred years, now is the time to
turn to Jesus Christ.

*~Let Us Be Ready~*

*I can do all things through Christ which strengtheneth me.*
*(Philippians 4:13 KJV)*

# ♥ Jesus IS Our Bonus ♥

May the God of hope fill you with all joy and peace in
believing, so that by the power of the Holy Spirit you
may abound in hope. (Romans 15:13 ESV)

So, it's pretty normal to look at other people and wonder
how they might have an easier life than you. How do
they have a bigger house, a newer car, a job that pays
large amounts of money, and they seem fit? Even
though we are commanded to not be envious, it's pretty
difficult to fight against our emotions. I, too, am not
perfect and can get caught up in the "envy" trap. But I
have a secret for you!

Even though some people seem to have a "perfect" life,
do they have Jesus? I have learned that even though I
don't have a big home or the nicest cars, am a stay-at-
home mom with zero income, and I go up and down
fifteen pounds like that is my job, I have Jesus. He is my
bonus in life that many other people don't have. Jesus is
more important than the things you seem to want but
cannot afford. If you want a bonus in life, turn to Him!

*~Love Your Life and Be Blessed to Know Jesus~*

*I can do all things through Christ which strengtheneth me.*
*(Philippians 4:13 KJV)*

# ♥ Grace Wins ♥

Let us then with confidence draw near to the throne of grace, that we may receive mercy and find grace to help in time of need. (Hebrews 4:16 ESV)

Stay alert and stay vigilant when it comes to your family's Spiritual growth. Continue to lead by example, even when it appears to go unnoticed. Planting seeds goes further in the souls of those we love than we know.

Abide in me, and I in you. As the branch cannot bear fruit of itself, except it abide in the vine; no more can ye, except ye abide in me. I am the vine, ye are the branches: He that abideth in me, and I in him, the same bringeth forth much fruit: for without me ye can do nothing. (John 15:4-5 KJV)

Even in times of anxiety and stress, stay close to Jesus and your family. Stay strong and communicate often. God is with you! His grace is yours.

But the God of all grace, who hath called us unto his eternal glory by Christ Jesus, after that ye have suffered a while, make you perfect, stablish, strengthen, settle you. (1 Peter 5:10 KJV)

*~When the Devil Goes Hard After your Family, You Go Harder After Jesus~*

*I can do all things through Christ which strengtheneth me.*
*(Philippians 4:13 KJV)*

# ♥*Life Changing Decision*♥

Therefore if any man be in Christ, he is a new creature: old things are passed away; behold, all things are become new. (2 Corinthians 5:17 KJV)

Change can be scary. But when we decide to turn to Jesus Christ, change is given a whole new meaning. It means we've decided to do what is right, what is true, and what is wise.

His path leads us to understanding what salvation truly is! We understand the consequences of our sins and what a true gift repentance actually is! Our eyes are open for the first time in our lives.

Change needs to take place in order to find His light; for He is the light of our world!

*~Find the Change You Need by Turning to Jesus~*

*I can do all things through Christ which strengtheneth me.*
*(Philippians 4:13 KJV)*

# ♥Say It Out Loud for Those in the Back♥

For we are his workmanship, created in Christ Jesus for good works, which God prepared beforehand, that we should walk in them. (Ephesians 2:10)

You are Loved!
You are Worthy!
You have Purpose!
You are Beautiful!
You are Special!
You have JESUS!

Life will be challenging for each and every one of us. This is just a fact! People will bully, scold, reject, and abuse you in one way or another. Do not ever succumb to the demons that others possess. We are given the power to not just love others, but to love ourselves. Go to God in every situation and be filled with His peace. His love for you will always prevail!

For I know the plans I have for you, declares the Lord, plans for welfare and not for evil, to give you a future and a hope. (Jeremiah 29:11 ESV)

*~You are Beautifully and Wonderfully Made~*

*I can do all things through Christ which strengtheneth me.*
*(Philippians 4:13 KJV)*

# ♥ *Love* ♥

Beloved, let us love one another, for love is from God,
and whoever loves has been born of God and knows
God. (1 John 4:7 ESV)

When I think about the word *love*, I think about the love
I have for my children. This form of love is pure,
selfless, giving, tender, disciplined, patient,
unconditional, real, vulnerable, centered, and
irrevocable. Nothing my children say or do could make
me love them less! There are times, however, when they
are rebellious and they turn away from my instruction,
but these are the challenges of parenting.

Now, think for a moment about the love that God has for
His children—us! His love for us is powerful and above
anything we could ever feel down here. Just as we love
our children, our God, our Father, has eternal love for
each of us. When we rebel and reject His instruction, He
hurts just as we do as parents. He worries just as we do.
His love for us is patient as He waits for us to return to
Him. He still loves us just as we still love our children!

Give thanks to the God of heaven, for his steadfast love
endures forever. (Psalm 136:26 ESV)

*~Love is Eternal~*

*I can do all things through Christ which strengtheneth me.*
*(Philippians 4:13 KJV)*

# ♥ He Will Protect You from the Evil One ♥

But the Lord is faithful, and will strengthen you and protect you from the evil one. (2 Thessalonians 3:3)

The evil one comes to destroy us. He lies, cheats, kills, and uses false scripture to lure us in to commit these evil acts. He is known as Satan! Do not be fooled by his deception.

Jesus comes to save, forgive, love, and lead us to the light of salvation.

Satan leads us to destruction, where we will not see the light at the end of our time.

Focus on the Lord at all times, and listen to guidance of the Holy Spirit.

*~Say No to Satan and Say Yes to Christ~*

*I can do all things through Christ which strengtheneth me.*
*(Philippians 4:13 KJV)*

# ♥ *Healing Powers* ♥

Therefore, confess your sins to one another and pray for one another, that you may be healed. The prayer of a righteous person has great power as it is working.
(James 5:16 ESV)

I'm a true believer in the healing power of prayer. I've seen it work in my life and in the lives of those I've prayed for. But understanding this power means that we must be willing to acknowledge that everything will happen in God's timing and in His own way. When we confess our sins to God and to those around us, we have opened up the way for our souls to be set free. Sin bears great burdens on our Spirits! And the good news is that we don't have to live this way. Confess, repent and let go.

Jesus answered them, "Truly, truly, I say to you, everyone who commits sin is a slave to sin. The slave does not remain in the house forever; the son remains forever. So if the Son sets you free, you will be free indeed". (John 8:34-36 ESV)

*~Confess, Repent and Let Go~*

*I can do all things through Christ which strengtheneth me.*
*(Philippians 4:13 KJV)*

# ❤ *Let Your Light Shine* ❤

Let your light shine before men, that they may see your good works, and glorify your Father which is in Heaven. (Matthew 5:16 KJV)

Letting our lights shine can sometimes take a tremendous amount of courage. We need the courage to stand in God's Holy Word! Through His Word we are to give, love, forgive, share, and glorify His name.

Our actions will always speak louder than our words. Our lights will shine brighter when we go out and help those in need, and when we take a path of righteousness to travel down. Let us pray, let us guide, and let us be active in shining our lights.

Again Jesus spoke to them, saying, "I am the light of the world. Whoever follows me will not walk in darkness, but will have the light of life." (John 8:12 ESV)

*~Shine in the Name of Jesus~*

*I can do all things through Christ which strengtheneth me.*
*(Philippians 4:13 KJV)*

# ♥When You Wake Up♥

My soul waits for the Lord more than the watchmen for the morning; Indeed, more than the watchmen for the morning. (Psalm 130:6 ESV)

When you wake up, what is the first thing you do? I typically talk to my five-year-old and get coffee. Sometimes I say good morning to God. Other times, I wake up feeling anxious about starting a new day of unknowns.

But today I woke up recognizing the need to pray and feeling the need to keep God as my center. When I opened my camera roll, there was Jesus as my first photo reminding me that He is with me and that I'm never alone.

The LORD is on my side; I will not fear: what can man do unto me? (Psalm 118:6 KJV)

Our fears, worries, and anxieties may be great, but our Lord is greater!

*~First Steps Every Morning~*

*I can do all things through Christ which strengtheneth me.*
*(Philippians 4:13 KJV)*

# ♥All Shapes and Sizes♥

Consider it pure joy, my brothers and sisters, [a] whenever you face trials of many kinds, because you know that the testing of your faith produces perseverance. Let perseverance finish its work so that you may be mature and complete, not lacking anything. (James 1:2-4 NIV)

Stress comes in waves of all shapes and sizes, and this stress can unfortunately blind us from enjoying life. I, for one, can recognize this stress when it starts to consume my mind by distracting me from living in the moment with my family. When this happens, I take a deep breath and pray to God, asking Him to help me through the struggle.

Once we recognize that we are distracted by stress, we are then able to give it to God. He is our comforter in our time of need.

Peace I leave with you, my peace I give unto you: not as the world giveth, give I unto you. Let not your heart be troubled, neither let it be afraid. (John 14:27 KJV)

*~God's Timing is Better than Ours~*

*I can do all things through Christ which strengtheneth me.*
*(Philippians 4:13 KJV)*

#  Devotion

Devote yourselves to prayer, being watchful and
thankful. (Colossians 4:2 NIV)

Devotion means to be loyal and dedicated, often times in
an act of prayer and worship. Here in Colossians 4:2, we
are told to devote ourselves to prayer. I certainly know
people who do not pray, even in times of trouble. If only
they could experience how truly life-changing it is! God
tells us that we must pray; He hears us.

Rejoice always, pray continually, give thanks in all
circumstances; for this is God's will for you in Christ
Jesus. (1 Thessalonians 5:16-18 NIV)

When we devote ourselves to our Lord, amazing things
happen. I have witnessed prayers being answered,
relationships being made stronger, fears and worries
fading, people helping one another, love conquering
hate, healing to the injured, inner pride turning to
humility, and family bonds and friendships being made
stronger!

This is the confidence we have in approaching God: that
if we ask anything according to his will, he hears us.
(1 John 5:14 NIV)

*~Pray, Watch and Give Thanks to our Lord~*

*I can do all things through Christ which strengtheneth me.*
*(Philippians 4:13 KJV)*

# ❤*Your Mindset is Your Own*❤

Peace I leave with you; my peace I give to you. Not as the world gives do I give to you. Let not your hearts be troubled, neither let them be afraid. (John 14:27 ESV)

Imagine for a moment a life without negative thoughts and without a complaining tongue. I, for one, have a very difficult time being around negative people. I found that no matter what I say or do, they find a reason to complain and a reason to be argumentative. God does not want this from us!

God's Word is purposed in providing understanding and peace to our unsettled hearts. With Lent approaching quickly, I have decided to give up all negative thinking and fill my words with encouragement for others to do the same.

As Jesus entered His forty days in desert, His complete trust and loyalty was to God to help Him through this fasting period and time of prayer. There is no mention in the Bible of Jesus complaining during this process. You see, when we keep God close and trust Him fully, He helps us through even our toughest struggles.

Let God's love and peace take over your complaining and negative hearts.

*~You can do it~*

*I can do all things through Christ which strengtheneth me.*
*(Philippians 4:13 KJV)*

# ♥ Use This ♥

When I sit and think about what I am most afraid of, I'm reminded that my fears are smaller than God's promises. Going out of my comfort zone is frightening for me. But I have reached a point in my life where I know I need to do something bold. My faith is not something I can bottle up and contain within the comfort of my home. My faith is meant to be shared, my voice is meant to be heard, and my physical and spiritual well-being is meant wear the full armor of God.

Use the Word of God to face your fears, challenges, and burdens. Use this to come out of your comfort zone to pursue the next steps of your journey. Use God's strength to be brave.

"Finally, be strong in the Lord and in his mighty power. Put on the full armor of God, so that you can take your stand against the devil's schemes. For our struggle is not against flesh and blood, but against the rulers, against the authorities, against the powers of this dark world and against the spiritual forces of evil in the heavenly realms. Therefore put on the full armor of God, so that when the day of evil comes, you may be able to stand your ground, and after you have done everything, to stand. Stand firm then, with the belt of truth buckled around your waist, with the breastplate of righteousness in place, and with your feet fitted with the readiness that comes from the gospel of

*I can do all things through Christ which strengtheneth me.*
*(Philippians 4:13 KJV)*

peace. In addition to all this, take up the shield of faith, with which you can extinguish all the flaming arrows of the evil one. Take the helmet of salvation and the sword of the Spirit, which is the word of God.

And pray in the Spirit on all occasions with all kinds of prayers and requests. With this in mind, be alert and always keep on praying for all the Lord's people." (Ephesians 6:10-18 NIV)

*~Life Shrinks or Expands in Proportion to One's Courage~*


# ❤You Are Always on God's Mind❤


How precious to me are your thoughts, God! How vast is the sum of them! Were I to count them, they would outnumber the grains of sand—when I awake, I am still with you. (Psalm 139:17-18 NIV)

His sole purpose is us! He created us out of love and therefore is with us always. When we choose to do good, He is pleased. When we choose to do evil, He is waiting for us to turn to Him. Go now and pray a prayer of thanksgiving to our Almighty Father in Heaven for His never-ending mercy and love.

*~Go Now and Turn to Our Lord~*

*I can do all things through Christ which strengtheneth me.*
*(Philippians 4:13 KJV)*

# ❤ Prayers for our Teachers and Children ❤

The prayer of a righteous person has great power as it is working. (James 5:16 ESV)

Dear Heavenly Father,

Today I pray for our children and teachers. I pray for their safety, and for their mental, physical, emotional, and spiritual well-being. Please guide and protect them in this new school year ahead. Help them to be respectful, gracious, and loving to one another's needs. I pray for appropriate disciplinary actions when needed to guide children down a path of righteousness. For you are a loving and merciful Father, so I pray these things in Jesus' name. Amen

*~Pray For Others Daily~*

# ❤ Blankets ❤

So we have come to know and to believe the love that God has for us. God is love, and whoever abides in love abides in God, and God abides in him.
(1 John 4:16 ESV)

So many people in our world are hurting. There seem to be blankets of sadness, stress, anxiety, and fear laying over our lands. And I know what so many of you are thinking—Where is God? After many years of living in

*I can do all things through Christ which strengtheneth me.*
*(Philippians 4:13 KJV)*

uncertainty and experiencing these similar, negative emotions, I've learned a few key points about our amazing Lord! My answer to this question is this...

The Rock, his work is perfect, for all his ways are justice. A God of faithfulness and without iniquity, just and upright is he. (Deuteronomy 32:4 ESV)

God is Love!
God is in Control!
God is with you through every struggle!
God is your biggest fan!
God is your comforter!
God answers prayers in His time and in His way!
God isn't a religion!
God is for everyone!
God forgives, heals, and stays with you always!
God is Sovereign!

We must Come out from under the blankets that continue to hold us down, fully understanding that we do not face our battles alone.

Fear not, for I am with you; be not dismayed, for I am your God; I will strengthen you, I will help you, I will uphold you with my righteous right hand.
(Isaiah 41:10 ESV)

*~Come Out From Under Your Blankets Wearing the Full Armor of God~*

*I can do all things through Christ which strengtheneth me.*
*(Philippians 4:13 KJV)*

# ♥ This Actually Works ♥

The Lord is my strength and my shield; in him my heart trusts, and I am helped; my heart exults, and with my song I give thanks to him. (Psalm 28:7 ESV)

Trusting in God actually calms your fears! I know this for two reasons.

1. The Bible tells us to trust Him.
2. When I close my eyes and tell God that I trust Him, my body immediately feels calm.

I'm terrified of heights. I was on a carnival ride with daughter, a Ferris wheel-type ride. These are the worst for me to ride, because they shake and get stuck at the top to let people on at the bottom.

My greatest fear came true when we kept getting stuck at the top, and we were the last people to be let off. My panic set in, and I was constantly complaining and hyperventilating.

As my daughter proceeded to laugh at my anxiety, the Holy Spirit reminded me to trust God. So, I closed my eyes and told God I trusted Him. My tight grip instantly loosened, and my body became calm. It was truly amazing!

Trust in the Lord with all your heart, and lean not on your own understanding. (Proverbs 3:5 NIV)

*~How Has Trusting God Helped You~*

*I can do all things through Christ which strengtheneth me.*
*(Philippians 4:13 KJV)*

# ❤*Disciples of Christ*❤

Go ye therefore, and teach all nations, baptizing them in the name of the Father, and of the Son, and of the Holy Spirit. (Matthew 28:19 KJV)

You can bless others through the name of Jesus Christ. You can read God's Word, follow it, and teach it to everyone you meet.

In fact, we are called to do just that. Have you tried it? It will be challenging and difficult at times, but God is with you through this journey.

All Scripture is breathed out by God and profitable for teaching. (2 Timothy 3:16 ESV)

*~Start Today~*

*I can do all things through Christ which strengtheneth me.*
*(Philippians 4:13 KJV)*

## Author's Bio

My name is Jennifer Taylor. As a young girl, I knew God was present in my life. I remember praying for world peace, although I never really understood what that meant, and also acknowledging that there was a constant presence around me. I became a mother at the age of 21 to my daughter, Audrey. Even then, I knew she as a gift from God. At the age of 23, after the birth of my second child, Danny, I was very busy and everyday life became a constant struggle. Yet, through it all, I still continued to pray.

Fast forward to age 36. I was now the mother of two more boys, Nathan and JT (James), and found myself remarried to a wonderful man. My children and I became members of an amazingly supportive church. This was where I heard that powerful call from the Holy Spirit telling me to start writing. I had been struggling with the idea of wanting to help people, but with four children and a tight budget, helping others seemed more like a dream than a reality. Little did I know that writing would be my way of helping others. The call was a soft yet precise voice, very distinct and exact in its message. Full of questions and doubt, I initially ignored my calling. The next month I heard it again, but this time it was in the form of a command. I followed its instruction and immediately began writing *Daily Devotions with Jen*.

I had fears of being ridiculed, blasphemed and hated for writing about God's Word. I then realized that, when

*I can do all things through Christ which strengtheneth me.*
*(Philippians 4:13 KJV)*

you are called to act on his behalf, you listen, follow and be brave.

God knew I was capable more than I knew myself. I knew that, given his instruction, and blessed with courage, I could go outside my comfort zone and proceed to this calling.

October 30, 2015, marks the first day of my writing journey. Through scripture I have been able to help others reaffirm their faith and hope in God's love for them. This journey has helped me understand that we are all called to ministry in one way or another. It is through us that God's word is taught, heard, obeyed and trusted.

Also I heard the voice of the Lord, saying, whom shall I send, and who will go for us? Then said I, Here am I; send me. (Isaiah 6:8 KJV)

Made in the USA
Columbia, SC
20 July 2023